Praise for *Bal*

"Jeanne McDermott captures the full...perience of a mother who loves a ba... ...from others and dependent for surviv... ...g edge medical treatment: the paralyzing fear that comes along with the unpredictable complications; the emotional ecology of life in the pediatric ICU; the way that worry and sadness can at one moment fray the bonds that bind parents to one another and at another moment bring estranged members of an extended family unimaginably close."
—Helen Featherstone, author of *A Difference in the Family*

"The gripping story of science writer and teacher McDermott's first year as the mother of a disabled child . . . filled with touching snapshots of Nathaniel's indomitable spirit and his parents' unflagging hope. . . . McDermott's courageous tale will prove riveting to most readers."
—*Kirkus Reviews*

"You will stay up all night to finish *Babyface: A Story of Heart and Bones*, but Jeanne McDermott's compelling memoir extends far beyond her own family's painful ordeal. It explores the pivotal moment that sooner or later divides everyone's lives into 'before and after.'"
—Ellen Kingsley, Editor-in-Chief, *ADDitude: The Happy, Healthy Lifestyle Magazine for People with ADD*

"This book artfully combines fact and feeling to illuminate how McDermott and her husband, Ted, dealt with the drastically altered circumstances of their lives. . . . Insightful and expressive."
—*Publishers Weekly*

"The literary grace of Jeanne McDermott transforms what begins as a harrowing story into a complex and ultimately inspiring tour through the intersection of science and fierce love. Readers of this book—may they be legion—will never encounter the words 'beauty' and 'normal' without recalling this mesmerizing read."
—George F. Will

PENGUIN BOOKS

BABYFACE

Jeanne McDermott has written for *Smithsonian, Horticulture, Elle, Popular Science, The Wall Street Journal,* and other publications and is the author of *The Killing Winds: The Menace of Biological Warfare.* She was a Knight Fellow in the Public Understanding of Science and Technology at MIT and holds a master's degree in teaching from Tufts University. Currently a science teacher, she lives in the greater Boston area with her husband and two children.

# Babyface

A
Story
of
Heart
and
Bones

Jeanne McDermott

PENGUIN BOOKS

PENGUIN BOOKS
Published by the Penguin Group
Penguin Putnam Inc., 375 Hudson Street,
New York, New York 10014, U.S.A.
Penguin Books Ltd, 80 Strand, London WC2R 0RL, England
Penguin Books Australia Ltd, 250 Camberwell Road,
Camberwell, Victoria 3124, Australia
Penguin Books Canada Ltd, 10 Alcorn Avenue,
Toronto, Ontario, Canada M4V 3B2
Penguin Books India (P) Ltd, 11 Community Centre,
Panchsheel Park, New Delhi – 110 017, India
Penguin Books (N.Z.) Ltd, Cnr Rosedale and Airborne Roads,
Albany, Auckland, New Zealand
Penguin Books (South Africa) (Pty) Ltd, 24 Sturdee Avenue,
Rosebank, Johannesburg 2196, South Africa

Penguin Books Ltd, Registered Offices:
Harmondsworth, Middlesex, England

First published in the United States of America
by Woodbine House Inc. 2000
Published in Penguin Books 2002

1   3   5   7   9   10   8   6   4   2

THE LIBRARY OF CONGRESS HAS CATALOGED
THE HARDCOVER EDITION AS FOLLOWS:
McDermott, Jeanne.
Babyface : a story of heart and bones / by Jeanne McDermott.—1st ed.
p.   cm.
ISBN 1-890627-15-1 (hc.)
ISBN 0 14 20.0033 7 (pbk.)
1. Head—Abnormalities—Patients—United States—Biography.
2. Face—Abnormalities—Patients—United States—Biography.
3. Disfigured children—United States—Biography.   I. Title.
RD763.M346   2000
362.1'9751043—dc21   [B]      99-087649

Printed in the United States of America
Set in Century Book

For Ganny

# Contents

# Acknowledgements

It always bears repeating that real life and a story are not the same thing. This string of words tries to capture some essential parts of life's rich adventure, but in the process of simplifying, dimensions of its mystery inevitably disappear. By taking a perspective, I've left others unexplored. All of the people involved in this story would tell something different than what I have chosen. One day, I hope that Nathaniel will tell his own. Responsibility for errors is mine. If I have misrepresented or portrayed anyone in a way that she or he finds hurtful, I apologize.

This book took a long time to write. In my case, writing is truly revision. It began with a journal kept during Nathaniel's first year of life and the story, written initially during naps and later between drop-off and pick-up, evolved from these scraps. The events in this book are true. The dialog was written not long after I heard it. For the sake of privacy, I changed many names. In a small number of scenes, I took the liberty of compressing two events that took place at slightly different times.

Books are never written alone. Some of my manuscript readers were anonymous but I would like to thank all those whom I know— including Alice Markowitz, Lynn McFarlan, Ted Finch, Jane Honoroff, Jay Wylie, Mary Beth Beale, Vivian Paley, Michael Congdon, Laura Van Dam, Kristen Wainwright, Alan Edelstein, and Peg Read. Their frank comments helped immeasurably at various stages along the way.

Many people were involved in the events of the story but, for the sake of narrative, are not mentioned. My deepest heartfelt thanks goes to Luci Fournier, Kit Bowry, Jennifer Burkin, Dottie MacDonald, Christine Sharry, Paul Solomon, Carol in Dr. Solomon's office, Deb Sieverson, Charlie Hergruetter, Dwight Jones, Kerry Jonely, Bonnie Blair, Martha Clifford, Miriam Lasher, June Cooperman, Ann Helwege, and Steve Moody. I would like to thank others who entered our lives after the main events of this story, including Debbie Sabin and the Lovelane Riding Program, Jennifer Kravitz, Debbie Packard, Jane Long, Susan Gordon, Lisa Diamant, Siobhan Doherty, Sharon Kingsbury, Rich Bruun, Bonnie Padwa, Steve Shusterman, Michael Williams, Cheonil Kim and all of Nate's hockey, soccer, and baseball coaches. To the many communities that have sustained us—Cambridge Montessori, Cambridge-Somerville Early Intervention, Wellesley Friends Meeting, Five Fields, Shady Hill— I offer my gratitude.

My appreciation for the staff at Children's Hospital Craniofacial Centre runs very deep. The dedication to taking care of children must be seen to be believed. Children's is my model for what every hospital could and should be.

Finally, I thank the staff of Woodbine House with a warm heart, for making a manuscript into the reality of a book. Thanks to Irv, Susan, and Fran, for your steadfast belief, kinship, humor, and most of all, your commitment to creating a more humane world.

To my family in all of its various incarnations—Finches, McDermotts, Woods, and all the steps, to dearly cherished friends, there would be no story without you. In the final analysis, your love, support, and presence makes all the difference.

# Introduction

※

Summer 1998

Just as there is art to giving a gift, so is there art to receiving, especially when the gift is unexpected. On a summer morning, tourists crowd the Tower of London, surging politely toward the ticket kiosks, speaking French, German, and Japanese. As Americans, we can understand the language, read the signs and decipher the prices, which are high. Two children clutch my hands as I inch along but when we finally reach the vendor, he signals us to wait and abruptly disappears. The children tug. What is he doing? Did the cash register run low? Has he sighted the suspicious-looking suitcase that terrorist bombers leave behind?

After five long minutes, the vendor returns and speaks to me discreetly: "I had to check with my superior." He slides our tickets through the window but also much more change than expected. The pound notes flutter between us, a puzzlement until he elaborates. "It's our law. Your child is disabled and you as the mother also get in for free."

I am pleased to have saved money but irritated about what must come next. Children watch adults very closely. Jeremy, our eleven-year-old, is waiting for an explanation. So is Nate who is seven and does not fathom why he would be responsible for this delay. But where to begin? Just this week, we had read a book about people with disabilities and when I asked Nate if he knew anyone who was disabled, he thought for a long time before giving the name of a boy who uses a wheelchair and another child who broke her arm. Disabled is not the way that Nate sees himself, nor the way that his family and friends see him. How does one tell children that we have no control over what single strand others choose to see in the multiple strands of our identities? This stranger in a faraway land has just given Nate a label and to complicate matters has handed over free tickets for the privilege.

"Thank you," I say quietly, before leading the children away.

∾

Later that summer, back in Boston where we live, Nate receives another unexpected gift at a Red Sox baseball game, but this one is much less complicated.

"Why did you bring your mitt?" asks Jeremy, who is strong, wiry, and eager to be cool. "You look like a dork."

Nate shrugs good-naturedly. His shorts are fashionably baggy but slightly askew. His hand-me-down T-shirt bears a few stains and his blond hair alternates between angelic curls and lion-mane dreadlocks. But unlike his brother, Nate couldn't care less about what he looks like. He's hoping to catch a ball.

It's family night at Fenway Park and we have seats on the third base line with a great view of the action. The Red Sox power hitter—Mo Vaughn—comes up to the plate, holding the baseball bat with arms that are as big as tree trunks. The day's heat stretches so deep into the night that even the darkness feels cozy. Ted and I hold hands, Jeremy studies each pitch intently, and Nate spies two empty seats in the front row.

"You want to go, Jay?" he asks his brother.

Jeremy shyly shakes his head, but Nate makes his way down, slipping in next to two middle-aged men who are barely watching the game. Instead, they pester the batboy from the visiting team, pleading every time he walks by. Mo gets on base, the next batter strikes out, and the inning fizzles but the fans don't give up, begging the batboy again and again until he finally reaches into his pocket and tosses them what they want. The middle-aged men whoop, holler, and sashay, elevating the object of their desire like a nugget of gold. Nate stares, unabashedly awestruck: A Real Major League Baseball!

The Ball circulates among the men, who rub it like the genie's magic lamp, but after the prize has been savored and shared, there is only one thing left to do. With infinite gentleness, the men turn to Nate and present the ball. It's impossible to gauge who is happier: the givers or the recipient. Nate holds the ball up in amazed delight for our inspection. We smile in return. Unlike the free tickets in London, there is nothing to explain about this gift, no discreet voice, no legalities, just the mutual joy and the spontaneous bond that the ball brings to everyone involved.

"He's so lucky!" Jeremy shakes his head in disbelief.

"He is," Ted acknowledges.

When the game ends, we amble back to the car, unconcerned that the Red Sox have lost or even that Mo had a bad night. Only in the car does Nate finally give the ball to Jeremy, who caresses the creamy leather, runs his fingers over the red stitching, and practices his curve ball grip, imagining himself on the mound.

As the car lurches out of the parking lot into the traffic, Nate contentedly sings, "I was born by the Fenway at Beth Israel Hospital." He pronounces it *Befizel*, one long word. Ted joins in, singing the lyrics to a Jonathan Richman song that my brother taught us long ago.

"I was almost born in the car," says Jeremy, who is embarrassed by these family singalongs.

"On the Boston University Bridge. At rush hour," says Ted.

"Was I almost born in the car?" Nate asks, his eyes drooping with sleep.

"No, thank God," I say quickly, remembering how unprepared we were for the package that Nathaniel came in.

"Tell me," Nate demands. "Tell me about when I was born."

"It's a long story," I reply.

# Babyface

every summer, our family takes a canoe trip. Last year we Looked on a map. We saw the rapids. we decided to Float down them. That day was as hot as the hottest desert. It felt great to be In the water.

(All writings by Nathaniel, age 9.)

# Chapter One

∾

# A Child

*Many years earlier—July 1990*

We had expected our second baby to be born fast. The morning that Nathaniel arrived, I woke with a contraction and Ted immediately sprang into action. He canceled his meetings, packed two bathing suits into the overnight bag, and shepherded me into the same car in which Jeremy, our first child, had nearly been born.

Jeremy had required little more than practiced hands to catch him, but he did join the world, much to our relief, in one of Boston's hospitals. Our panicky drive had coincided with rush hour, and was leavened by one comic moment when I lifted my head off the back seat, saw Ted mired in traffic, and wondered if it was logistically possible to give birth with pants on. Birth is a natural process, but then so are hurricanes, epidemics, and

the bites of black widow spiders, and it had seemed fool-
ish to be stranded in a car over the Charles River without any medical back-up.

The second time around, we planned to get to the
hospital with time to spare, and at least take advantage
of the comforts advertised on the tour of Beth Israel's
maternity floor. Ted harbored romantic visions of listening to soothing jazz, pacing the halls arm in arm, and
soaking in the hot tub, which, even in the humidity of
July, sounded like an infinitely better place to go through
labor than the back seat of our car.

By nine a.m., Jeremy had settled into nursery school
and we began the fifteen-minute drive from Cambridge
to Boston, with a smug sense of satisfaction. As Ted nosed
into a rotary, a contraction jack-hammered my body,
shortly followed by another even more intense, leaving
me slumped in the front seat, humbled and
hyperventilating.

"Which way?" Ted pleaded. I cracked my eye, feebly
waved a finger, and Ted veered off onto one of many spokes.

"That way!" I screamed with a sickening sense of
deja vu that this was where we had gotten lost on our
last mad dash.

Ted regained his sense of direction just in time. The
hospital loomed beyond a mess of buses, through which
Ted deftly maneuvered. When we reached the front entrance, the security guard took the car keys. From the shadows, Ted commandeered a wheelchair and firmly took
charge, relaying names, addresses, and health insurance
information to a nearby nurse. We crowded onto a waiting
elevator, where the red numbers very slowly blinked on
and off and, to Ted's chagrin, I bellowed like an injured
animal, past caring about anybody or anything. Ted was
not ready to concede, but I knew that the baby had won.

When the elevator opened at the maternity floor, a
nurse grabbed the handles, the linoleum floor rushing

past the wheelchair's footrests in a blur. After the contraction ended, I looked up, disappointed by the Spartan delivery room, with its beige bed, beige chair, and Wizard of Oz drape concealing the emergency equipment. The one window, which offered a bleak view of a parking lot, only enhanced the budget motel ambiance; decoration unworthy of the room's grand purpose.

But the next contraction wiped out any sensitivity to my surroundings. Ted grasped how far and how fast labor had progressed when I could not heave myself onto the bed without his steadying grip around my shoulders. A twinge of disappointment registered on his face but that gave way to glee as the nurse midwife expertly belted an elastic monitor around my aching belly.

"You can see the heartbeat!" Ted said excitedly.

I squinted at the dark computer screen looming next to the bed where the white zig-zags of my heartbeat chased the baby's. Lub-dub and I made strong, playful leaps and at the same time, electronically beeped, like an alarm gone berserk. Ted squeezed my hand as I closed my eyes to ride out the next contraction.

"Open, remember?" he prodded kindly when the pain ended. He meant my eyes. I had seen nothing during Jeremy's birth because all of the medical rigmarole—the machines, monitors, gowns, IVs, even stethoscopes—infused me with terror. It was one of those professional ironies that inspired guffaws: I was a science journalist with seemingly endless curiosity about how things worked, yet squeamish about my own body. With the simple trick of shutting my eyes, the fear vanished and with the fear gone, pain became manageable but Ted had felt left out.

"I'll try. Remind me if I forget," I said, blocking out everything in the delivery room except Ted. Looking at the heartbeat monitor was bad enough. Unlike Ted, who saw merely numbers, I replayed every delivery room horror story in my expansive repertoire. I could not help second-guessing the dire circumstances indicated nor could I stop worrying that the nurse midwife had missed a vital detail every time she glanced in the other direction. So I clung to Ted's green eyes, captivated by their perfectly compatible promise of safety and adventure and the knowledge that he would have given anything to change places, not from any heroic sense of duty but because he would have liked to experience childbirth himself.

I had known Ted a long time. We met in college when he climbed a ladder propped next to my dorm window and offered to share a box of strawberries—a sweet exchange that foreshadowed many more. While Ted studied wind energy and I concentrated on microbiology, a friendship grew which blossomed into romance after graduation, and, in due course, marriage. Having left windmills behind for business school, Ted now worked at an investment firm in Boston as a stock analyst.

The pain intensified, jerking the muscles in my body, dimming the sweet glow between us. As the lull between contractions shrank, so did my capacity for rational thought until primal instinct took over, annihilating all senses of boundary and definition. I sweated, got chilled, and became furious with Ted for not divining each thought as it passed through my mind at breakneck speed. As Ted put socks on my freezing feet, I wanted to push but hesitated, not trusting that this baby was ready to be born so soon.

A pit crew of nurse midwives and doctors migrated from other posts on the maternity floor and with authoritative voices reassured that now was the time. Summoning all of my strength, I pushed but a rational thought intruded: this was much more strenuous than what Jeremy had required. That registered as wrong. I suppressed panic and redoubled my efforts on the next command, chiding myself that every baby is different, and yet oddly aware that emergencies require calm and speed. I forced my eyes open, searching for Ted's confidence to rein the growing fear back.

"Scream if it helps," he urged.

I let out a sharp yell as the next contraction hit.

"Again," he said, trying to veil his pain at seeing my own.

"No, it makes it worse."

There was no time to say more as voices coached and cajoled, and then suddenly the baby slid out. What exhilarating triumph, what giddy joy, what hard labor to birth a child! Breathless, I glanced up at the wall clock. It read 10:30. Only an hour after arriving at the hospital, I thought. I ached to meet the little being who voyaged from beyond. Having once experienced the magical, boundlessly hopeful sense that only a newborn can bring, I waited eagerly, impatient to experience it again.

The room swelled with rosy silence, no words, just happy panting as Ted joined the doctors and nurses huddled at the base of the bed, doing the Apgar Test behind the curtain. With the worst over, I was not worried. It had taken a little while for Jeremy to breathe at first. Then Ted returned and his hand tensed in mine, communicating a problem that was obvious and visible to everyone in the room, except me.

The baby was in trouble.

What did that mean? Something cold sliced through my joy. I felt accelerating fear, a dark funnel of unvoiced thoughts and feelings, a concentration of a purpose, people jostling in and out, the absence of our baby's cry, the agony of not being able to see this new little person. Finally, someone said, "We're having trouble getting him to breathe. He needs to go to intensive care."

"Can't I hold him?" I asked. "Just for a minute?"

Ted's eyes widened behind his glasses as he whispered that the baby's fingers were fused and something about the bones in his head and face had not formed right. When the doctor nervously placed the minute-old baby in my arms, Ted circled us both in a tightening embrace. Deep shock brought an exaggerated calm in the moment that I touched the baby's hands. They looked like mittens! A tiny thumb was separate but pearly skin joined the other fingers together, making little pink cups.

*That's no big deal*, I thought with a flash of intuition. Ted gently stroked the baby's tall bulging head, felt the bumpy ridge above his eyes that made him look as if he had worn a tight hat whose band had left its mark. Only when the baby's rosy mouth puckered into a soundless cry did I understand as clearly as Ted had just minutes earlier that, for his survival, the doctors must take this extraordinary baby away.

While the placenta was delivered, a resident asked, "What's the baby's name?"

The simple question summoned the biggest uncertainty that had preceded his birth. "We were going to name him Nathaniel. But maybe he is a Gabriel?"

"Why?" Ted held my gaze.

"He'll need his guardian angel," I declared, eyes brimming, unable to say that since everything we imagined for this baby had changed, maybe his name should too.

Ted shook his head, sympathetically. The fear in his eyes dissolved into a passionate clarity that said he had bonded to this child as instantaneously as I had.

"No," Ted said in a quietly reassuring voice. "He is Nathaniel. The Nathaniel we have been waiting for."

Then it ended. The men and women who attended the birth filed slowly out, shoulders slanting, faces shadowed, dodging any direct gaze. A taut silence stretched across the delivery room. Only one, the last to leave, gently murmured, "congratulations," the single word that the others had not voiced. My anger boiled like magma. I hated the strangers who had glimpsed our baby's first battles for breath and yet greeted his entry into the world without joy, welcome, or encouragement.

Then as quickly as it boiled, the anger subsided while Ted and I clung to each other, tears raining down our cheeks. A healthy boy: the amnio had promised, that's what we had announced exuberantly to my parents in Chicago, to his in New York, to brothers, sisters, and scattered friends, that's all that had ever mattered. Now our healthy baby boy lay in intensive care and his absence brought a searing animal pain, infinitely more excruciating than labor.

For nine months—settling behind the steering wheel, rolling over in bed, bending down—I had been obsessed with the baby's well-being, aware that every sip, every bite, every chance to put my feet up had been for him. Now I wanted nothing more than to safeguard him as I had for nine months. Here in the hospital, when he most needed to be protected, I had failed. Ted was quietly torn between taking care of me and going to intensive care. Please, please go, I urged him, pleased that he could do what I could not, but as soon as he vanished down the wide unfamiliar hallway, I wished him back.

Abandoned in the delivery room, I lay on the hospital bed, haunted by a suddenly vivid nightmare. Last night, I had dreamt of taking a trip and found myself in labor, in the countryside far from home, in a squalid, rat-infested hospital where bare bulbs lit cinder block walls, like the Godforsaken Rumanian orphanages depicted in magazine exposes. I refused to have the baby, saying, "There is no neo-natal intensive care unit."

I opened my eyes and looked out the window, scanning the uneasy blue sky above the parking lot. I tried to shake off the memory as a disturbing coincidence. In a hallucinatory moment, I floated, detached from my body, suspended in the void of nothingness. Fascinated by the unfamiliar sensations of hyperawareness, my attention pirouetted around the room. The textures flattened, the already mute colors became even more indistinct, the flat surfaces of wall, floor, and ceiling undulated while utter quiet descended like a bell jar. The room became strangely peaceful, the loneliness welcome. Only the phone, next to the bed, exerted a frightening presence. The act of speaking, explaining, or elaborating on what had just happened defied comprehension. Complicated thoughts splintered into fragments which no language could encompass.

I struggled to get my bearings, imagining shreds of a previous life, but unable to see the connection between our three-year-old son, Jeremy, on the nursery school playground and our newborn in intensive care. There was a link between this morning and now but since the connection was too remote to grasp, too ephemeral to find, I stared instead at the tiny dancing bubbles of carbonation inside the glass of ginger ale next to the bed. As each bubble burst with a pop, releasing a spray and then diffusing into the air, I felt an unaccountable kinship and sense of wonder as if I was pushing my way through the sugary liquid, breaking the surface tension and soaring freely away.

A wary nurse intruded into the room, speaking words hard to translate, trying to help me change my clothes. Too much had been taken, too permanently, too fast and I was shaking my head, refusing the hospital johnny. I needed to wear the T-shirt that I had borrowed from Ted earlier in the morning, for a token of protection, the ghostly droop of his shoulders around my own. But Ted saved me when he burst back into the delivery room, eyes bright with discovery, accompanied by a doctor who solemnly carried a dog-eared textbook.

"We think that your son has a craniofacial abnormality," the doctor said, with a cough as he pointed to a stark, black and white photograph of a boy with bulging eyes, towering head, and slack-jawed mouth.

"But you're not sure," I said, feeling a surge of manic lucidity, the intellectual equivalent of the mother who hoists the car off her child.

"We are trying to find someone in the hospital who has seen a child with Apert syndrome before," he acknowledged, awkwardly pronouncing "AY-pert" as if he had never heard the word actually spoken.

Apert syndrome. Whoever the hell Dr. Apert was. I despised the cold hollow sound of the diagnosis, the sliver of immortality that it conferred on a stranger whose scientific calling had culminated not in the naming of an Alpine peak, lunar valley, or Amazonian orchid but this claim to my child. Nathaniel would never belong to Dr. Apert or anyone else, but the name meant that he inhabited the known world and for that small favor I could see that Ted was very grateful.

The boy on the page stared implacably back. When I had glimpsed a similar photo in college, I had averted my gaze but now I studied the image with stunned fascination. The aggressive mug-shot pose made the boy a specimen. In my mind's-eye, I resurrected his humanity by conjuring a teddy bear and muddy sneakers outside of the picture's frame until I was wrenched by the realization that I had seen this face more recently in the studio of my friend, the photographer Nancy Burson.

Nancy and I had met five years earlier when I interviewed her for a magazine article on—oddly enough—the face. She had recently begun a new project photographing children born with rare craniofacial conditions. Confronted by the medical picture, I could not avoid the sense that in a conspiracy of forces beyond my control, Nancy had been guiding me, long before this day. Then this glimpse of order evaporated like a thread of smoke and I was jarred back to the chaotic present.

"When can I see him?" I asked, urgently.

"When his condition is stable. Nathaniel is having a hard time breathing on his own. Probably because the bones in his nose did not form properly," the doctor explained as he wheeled me out of the delivery room to make way for another child ready to be born.

∾

As Ted made the first phone calls, I loved him fiercely and wondered from what unknown place he found the poise, composure, and gentle voice to announce that Nathaniel had arrived but was in intensive care. He called someone who became so distraught and hysterical that across the room, I could hear the voice urging Ted to let Nature take its course.

"He's not a vegetable," Ted said calmly.

There was a pause.

"He's not going to die," Ted said.

Another pause.

"They're not prolonging his suffering. He had a hard time breathing. He's getting oxygen."

Across the room, the voice said doctors are arrogant assholes who do what they damn well please, forget the heroics.

"Nathaniel is fine," Ted soothed before hanging up. "They're giving him extra help. That's all."

While Ted paced, drained, I reached my younger brother Charlie's answering machine and after hearing his upbeat message, paused idiotically and then sobbed. I repeated this performance with Dad's answering machine in Chicago.

"The baby's here," I choked out the news to Mom's housekeeper when she said Mom was out. "Tell Mom ..." Tell Mom what? "Tell Mom that he's got problems."

"Honey," she said with serenity. "We've all got problems."

"Not like this," I replied.

∾

I had never been in intensive care, much less one for infants. As soon as Nathaniel stabilized in the afternoon, I followed the directions written in bold letters, washed my hands at the stainless steel sink, and nervously entered a sunny space fully equipped—with every life-enhancing gizmo and gadget—to handle the most dire circumstances of a child's arrival into the world.

So finally! This was our baby!

But he seemed lost in a seaweed of tubes, swallowed up by computers that displayed his heartbeat and every other vital function, engulfed by a dataflow larger than his body. Every aspect of intensive care—from the deathly calm to the mission control equipment—repulsed me except its purpose. I opened my eyes, searched Ted's for reassurance, but found none.

Nathaniel lay on a table-high incubator, not swaddled, but under the glow of heat lamps, warmed like a dish in a restaurant kitchen. The tiny oxygen mask, the suction tube in his mouth, the IV in his ankle, the round heart monitor patched on his chest, the red light of the oxygen monitor taped to the pellucid skin of his big toe—the technology was comprehensible yet opaque. I understood what it was doing but not why.

I sought a place to touch Nathaniel, reaching under the heat of the incubator light for his tiny mitten hand. As soon as I placed one finger inside his smooth palm, tears brimmed in my eyes. With the other hand, I stroked his scrawny leg, wrinkled from the amniotic bath, his translucent skin criss-crossed with purply veins and covered with sworls of downy hair, noticing for the first time that his little toes were webbed too.

"Did you see that?" I nudged Ted.

He nodded and said with delectable surprise, "He's so big."

I bent over the plastic crib, whispering in his tiny ear. "Hey, little guy. I'm so sorry that you have to be here." Nathaniel startled and returned to dreamy oblivion.

"How will they ever fix that?" I stroked Nathaniel's clotted masses of black hair. His forehead seemed enormous, his brow bulging and folding above his eyes, as if the middle of his face had been stamped down.

The NICU doctor shook his head and promised that if anyone knew the answers to our questions, it would be the craniofacial specialist at Boston's Children's Hospital, who planned to visit at the end of the day.

Ted sighed deeply, for no remedy was obvious. Watching Nathaniel breathe, his mouth open, sucking air noisily, his tongue periodically defeating the whole effort, terrified Ted. He had already witnessed him turn dusky blue, once at birth and once in the aftermath.

"When I was in medical school, the textbook said that babies are nose breathers," explained the NICU doctor, sounding like a ship captain talking about a malfunctioning bilge pump. "In forty years here, I've seen kids born without a nose. This guy doesn't have a choice either. He'll figure it out."

He said that Nathaniel also had pneumothoraxes, little pockets of air trapped between the lung and the chest cavity, which made his breathing problems even worse.

"It happens sometimes when babies are born fast," shrugged the NICU doctor, suggesting that he had seen more than we would ever guess. "This guy came fast, didn't he?"

Ted nodded, appalled by how hard it was for Nathaniel to do what most newborns do effortlessly.

"How's he going to nurse?" I asked, longing for the bond of breastfeeding to ease the terrors.

"Babies were made so they don't need to eat for the first 48 hours anyway. He'll have to eat and then breathe. Take turns."

It seemed unfathomable but the NICU doctor's allegiance and faith in the tiny babies for whom he was responsible quieted my doubts and eased the furrows on Ted's brow.

"Give him more time," urged the NICU doctor. "He's had a rough morning."

"How many kids have you seen with Apert syndrome?" Ted asked.

"This makes—let me see—three," he hazarded.

Three in forty years, at a city hospital where a baby was born every hour of the day and night? I shook off the NICU's numerical obsessions and stared at Nathaniel, wondering again who this baby would be. Common sense dictated that a second child would be different. I had wished for a child with Ted's full lips and strong Yankee jaw, my black Irish eyes and long neck, knowing that no one can predict what rogue gene will gain the upper hand.

When Jeremy was born, I saw a baby lucky to have college-educated parents who lived in a democracy where sewage treatment and mandatory vaccination promised a long life. Nathaniel occupied the same demographic niche as his brother but because his hands and face—the two parts of anatomy most closely identified with being human—were different, doubt swaddled his future.

"That number went below 90. It's not supposed to go below 90. What was that?" Ted asked when an alarm blasted.

The nurse quickly checked it and answered, "Bad connection in the circuit."

15

∾

When Jeremy came to the hospital at the end of the day to meet his little brother, his simple innocence ignited the joy shrouded by the syndrome, interventions, and the things gone wrong. After performing the ritual ablutions at the entrance with an expertise that I hated having acquired so quickly, I led Jeremy into the intensive care unit. He giggled, ignored the medical hardware, and took no notice of the preemies in their isolette spaceships struggling to survive.

"Say hi," Ted said, hoisting Jeremy up so that he could peek into his new baby's crib. Jeremy gently patted Nathaniel's head and then wiggled out of Ted's embrace, eager to test-drive one of the rocking chairs that circulated around the NICU.

"You want to hold him? You can," Nathaniel's nurse said to me. "He's been doing great!"

"I'd love to," I replied and then asked quickly, "How about you, Ted?"

"Sure," he said a smile blossoming across his etched face.

"You go first," I said, suddenly afraid.

The nurse settled Nathaniel, who had wires and tubes coming out of him like a stereo, in Ted's arms. Ted adjusted the little knit cap, too tight for his big head, then quieted Nathaniel's whimpers with the same nurturing clucks that soothe a high-strung horse.

"Here, Jeremy," I said. "Let's tape your letter to Nathaniel's crib."

Ted had taken dictation: "Dear Baby—I love you and see you everyday. I will talk to my mom and then I will open my big brother presents and then I will go sailing and then I'll go to the haircut place and then I'll see you in the morning and that's it. Love, Jeremy."

"How about your baby present?" I asked.

Jeremy happily dropped a terry-cloth Babar rattle inside the crib, where the red light of the disconnected oximeter illuminated the King of the Elephant's dignified, merciful face. Why sailing? I wondered. Where did he pick that up?

Then, Ted and I switched places. For a brief second at Nathaniel's birth, I had cradled him, but not truly supported the weight of his wrinkled body nor fully absorbed his musky scent. Now, despite the electronics, I savored the bliss of a warm new life pulsing in my arms. In the family snapshot taken by friends that first night, sorrow tugged at the corner of Ted's mouth, Jeremy's limbs blurred, Nathaniel slept, and I smiled, buoyed with daffy optimism—our baby was born, he was alive and all the rest would work out.

By nine o'clock, after the summer sun had set, Jeremy rested his head on Ted's sagging shoulder, both looking exhausted, I thought with regret.

"I love you," Ted said, kissing me goodbye. "Get some sleep."

I murmured the same as he staggered to the elevator and I retreated to the blueish dark of my hospital room, where the breadth and amplitude of the day began to sink in. In the thick of Nathaniel's medical issues, I had forgotten what it meant to recover from childbirth. But body pain was inconsequential compared to the demons that danced in my imagination, thwarting sleep.

"I saw your light," the night nurse said, after knocking softly on my door. "How are you?"

"I'm scared that Nathaniel will live at home forever," I sniffled. "I'm scared that kids will tease him and no one will invite him to a birthday party."

She sat on the edge of the bed, quickly reached over, and hugged me with big soft arms, her blue hospital smock absorbing the tears. "I saw him in the nursery.

He's big! And cute. There's a girl who lives across from me—I think she's got the same thing. She's at the local high school."

"Really?"

"You'll be amazed."

"He's not the baby I imagined," I sighed. "I'll go upstairs and hold him. That's the only thing that makes me feel better."

The night nurse opened the door onto a corridor dark and lonely as a city street, except for a light at the end of the hall where a policeman, arms folded across his stocky chest, sat in a folding chair outside one of the rooms.

"What's the cop doing?" I asked.

"Working," she paused. "I'm not supposed to say this but one of the mothers is an inmate from Framingham. Don't stay too long. Try to get some sleep."

In the NICU, I took Nathaniel out of the incubator myself and we rocked and rocked and rocked while blue-suited nurses measured the progress of tiny lives, in a cloying fog of alcohol and disinfectant. I stared numbly out the dark window at Boston. Above the lights that craned over Fenway Park, lightning split the sky and thunder boomed like fireworks as storms churned their way towards the Atlantic. It was a city where common sense had never gone out of style and where a social revolution had been born based on the radical but necessary lie that we are all created equal. The local radio station played a popular hit from the 1970s. "Of all the dreams I've lost and found," sang Joan Baez. Of all the dreams. Nathaniel stirred and I brushed him with tears. In the hourless depths of the night, in the predawn NICU, I grieved for the dreambaby who had died and loved the one who had been born.

I Like to build with K'nex. I built a solar-powered flying machine. One day after Cub Scouts, my friend and I made a huge blimp together. We made a flat-bed carrier for it to ride on.

# Chapter Two

❧

# Homecoming

July 1990

All things considered, the eve of the twenty-first century was not the worst time in history to be born with a craniofacial syndrome. Although one doctor did ask if we wanted to give Nathaniel up for adoption, no one suggested that he get fed to the wolves, buried alive to appease the gods, condemned to sideshows, treated as a curse, or even labeled a monster. He escaped the equally unthinkable destinies of those born in previous generations whose parents had been told that they should put the child away. *Away*? I shuddered to imagine Nathaniel automatically shunted to a state-run human warehouse.

In 1990, in a big, forward-thinking Boston hospital, the staff was prepared to help not only the babies who had special needs but the families too. A social worker counseled us in the NICU about the twists and turns ahead. As she registered Nathaniel for the Cambridge Early Intervention Program and plied us with brochures about medical insurance and Massachusetts's special needs services, Ted and I joked about whether Nathaniel qualified for the hard-to-get handicapped parking sticker.

But our laughter was apprehensive. A quick glance at the past reaffirmed the truth that the human body was life's vessel and its shape, color, or components charted the course of destiny in profound and capricious ways. Western leaders had long relied on "scientific" explanations about what was "biological" and thus "natural" to justify a long and depressing list of cultural inequity, disenfranchisement, and horror: Hitler targeted the disabled as the first to die in his genocidal quest to create a master race, members of the United States Congress debated what fraction of personhood should be allotted to African slaves, and women were denied the right to vote or own property because uteruses rendered them constitutionally weak.

Science had changed, but who would the turn-of-the-century American culture acknowledge Nathaniel to be? In a nation of immigrants who had a history of reinventing themselves in the pursuit of perfect happiness, the body was a battleground for contradictory cultural messages. While the mass media created its own unattainable standards of beauty—idolizing thin young bodies as rare as Nathaniel's syndrome—it also promoted indiscriminate consumption. The result was cultural schizophrenia—a nation of overweight, fast-food junkies who suffered from an epidemic of eating disorders and flocked to plastic surgeons and diet doctors. In an era of unprecedented longevity and public health, it was strangely paradoxical how few Americans actually seemed content in their own skin.

After four days, Nathaniel left the hospital. His homecoming felt like a singular and monumental achievement but in retrospect, it proved to be merely the first of many. The events of the next year transformed the crazy quilt of family, our perceptions of difference, and beliefs about what it means to be human. Loving Nathaniel demanded a whole new way of seeing, not simply him and others, but ourselves.

But all that lay in the future. On the first ride home from the hospital, I had the sobering realization that our uncertainties had only just begun. The world out there, beyond the controlled walls of the hospital, would not be as welcoming nor as informed. How would people respond to Nathaniel? How would he be treated? Ted and I were enough products of the 1960s to embrace the social activism that a child like Nathaniel would need, but the prospect of battling for his civil rights came so soon after fighting to keep him alive, that I wondered where we would find the strength.

Ted swung the car into the driveway of our two-family house on a quiet Cambridge side street. My mother waved a teary welcome from the front stoop. I climbed the stairs slowly to the second and third floors where we lived, not recognizing the ruthlessly clean living room, the crumbless tablecloth, ironed napkins, and gleaming sink faucets. Even the usually empty glass shelves in the refrigerator bulged with casseroles and soups.

Mom had been busy. At sixty-five, she had buoyant energy on and off the tennis court, a cheerful, gregarious temperament, and a well of belief that things usually worked out for the best. Her talent for vaporizing clutter, like her work as a historian, was a late-life phenomenon. She was a child who had rebelliously shoved her junk in the closet when her father made his monthly inspection, an off-hand parent who had imposed few rules while raising three kids. In fact, I had often mothered her as a child, picking up the slack when she was overwhelmed by my active older brother, when she and my father divorced, when she remarried a man 25 years her senior.

"Let the machine answer," Mom sighed as the phone rang, her usual optimism depleted.

"Everybody is offering to help." She flipped open a spiral notebook where she had written names, phone numbers, and messages in the same neat cursive that she shared with her mother and two sisters. "They need to help. Be specific, whether it is food, errands, or making calls. Let me tell you: it gets old quick saying the same things over and over."

Even casual conversations about Nathaniel quickly turned into biology lectures. The pediatric cardiologist had discovered that Nathaniel had tiny holes inside the chambers of his heart, ventricular septal defects he called them, that allowed blood to leak where it shouldn't go. The hand surgeon had explained that the separation of his fingers, or as he said, *syndactyly release*, required skin grafting, casts, and multiple microsurgeries staged over many years. The craniofacial surgeon had declared that three of the bones in Nathaniel's skull had fused prematurely, along the saggital, lamboidal, and coronal sutures—(where were they were all located?)—and should be fixed by surgery, which he'd be happy to discuss at our next appointment.

In the dazed expression on my face, Mom read that it was a burden to think—let alone think ahead. I wanted our friends to do what they had always done— be there, shoot the breeze, pass the time. But the unfairness of the situation slammed me and I wondered, *why* wasn't this second child easier? We were supposed to be competent, prepared, and knowledgeable, so why weren't our friends?

Dressed in a diaper and a doll-sized undershirt, Nathaniel looked like a sticky comma as he slept in a car seat on top of the kitchen counter. His world consisted of hunger and sleep, lights and shadows, the drama of a baby's simple emotions. Because his eyelids didn't close all the way, he gave the impression that he was half listening. He had no clue that he was physically different and for years to come, he would not. He would learn to see himself as all babies did—by the way that others responded to his presence. Babies needed to be adored, cooed over, and delighted in. That was his birthright: nothing more and nothing less.

"I want people to welcome this child," I said with welling urgency and then quickly amended. "I want people to love him."

"He's a miracle," Mom declared, looking at me and then Nathaniel with flinty pride, not the helpless fright that had clouded her eyes in the NICU, when I sobbed because I could not breathe for him and she sobbed because she could not breathe for me.

"What do you mean?" I asked. Sometimes Mom's idea of a miracle was finding just the right outfit to wear.

Her eyes blazed, "Why he brought me and your father and step-mother together!"

"How?" I asked, genuinely perplexed.

My parents' relationship had the structural tensions of a long-span bridge. The only thing trickier than having a newborn in intensive care had been having everyone collide there. Mom had not forgiven Dad for the dissolution of their marriage twenty years earlier. Every time my brothers and I pointed out that this too had been for the best, she got a stubborn look and refused to budge.

"We hugged and cried, the three of us," Mom said quietly.

"Together? In my hospital room?" I sputtered, revising my notion that Nathaniel's first time nursing had been the day's momentous event.

Mom nodded as she took a sponge to a small spot of grease at the edge of the stove that had escaped her quest.

It was funny to see that order was her reaction to the anarchy of the last few days.

"Amazing," I said, impressed. If Nathaniel had already in his short life created a bond conspicuously absent from twenty years of family events—what more to expect?

"Let's start a schedule then," said Mom, briskly rinsing out the sponge as she turned her attention from the miraculous to the mundane. "Who's Albert?"

"He works with Ted."

"Can he drop by tonight?"

"OK."

"I'll set another place at the table. Now you sit down," she ordered.

I lugged Nathaniel's car-seat downstairs to the backyard, set it on the shady ground and climbed into the hammock stretched between the ash and pear trees, dozing off. The last four days had been so preternaturally long that I half expected the seasons to have changed. In our neighborhood, summer meant no privacy. The houses were so close that when the child next door cried from nightmares, I awoke, sure that the sobs came from ours.

We had lived here for five years. When the house came on the market the day before our wedding, Ted fell in love with what it might become, especially the garden. I balked and pronounced it boring—my way of saying that getting married and buying a house in the same forty-eight-hour period required more sanity than I had. Fortunately, it ran against Ted's grain to pass up a good opportunity, even if the timing was inconvenient.

The garden gate creaked as Ted came back from next door, where he had collected Jeremy, who was the same age as our neighbor's child, Ben. The two boys diffused between backyards, while we helped each other out with baby-sitting on the weekends.

"What happened, Mr. Peanut?" I asked. He also answered to Jay, J-J, Jay Bird, Peanut, and Pea as well.

"We have a problem," Ted said, with a grim look that meant Big Problem. Jeremy jumped out of his embrace and scooted off to the sandbox while Ted sank, flabbergasted, into the hammock.

"The boys ..." he started.

"What?"

"Oh God," Ted exhaled.

"What happened?" I pressed.

"Jeremy hit Ben," he said.

"It isn't the first time," I said evenly.

"It happened before I got there but Paula does not want them near each other. Not just today but from now on." Paula was Ben's mother.

"Why?" My stomach pitched.

"Paula was sick and tired of Ben being a punching bag. She thinks that Jeremy needs therapy."

Mom appeared next to the hammock, with a glass of water, her expression of protective concern signaling that she had overheard.

"So what should we do?" I whispered, wishing immediately that Ted had asked someone else to take care of Jeremy while we were at the hospital. As if that would have prevented this scene! But how could he have known? Jeremy was singing to himself in the sandbox, the picture of serenity as he smoothed a road with his big brother present, a yellow backhoe.

"Nothing right now. They're leaving tomorrow to go on vacation for two weeks," Ted said.

Nathaniel's head slumped in the car seat. His tongue got in the way and he wheezed and rattled like a broken air conditioner. The hospital crash course in infant CPR had left Ted confident that he could resuscitate a doll. While he maneuvered Nathaniel, propping his head first this way and then that, I rehearsed what to do if he turned blue, ready to sprint him to the nearby fire station for a whiff of oxygen.

"And she had to tell you—the parents of a newborn who can't breathe—this news? Today?" Mom shook her head in protective outrage.

"Do you think Jeremy needs therapy?" I worried.

"We all need help." Mom's bark said I was being ridiculous. "You know, this isn't about Jeremy."

I looked up in the hemlock tree just outside our bedroom window where the screeching sound of raccoons fighting filled the night. So this was our homecoming?

"But the food that Paula brought over?" Ted offered gently.

"She snapped," Mom said.

"It's too much," Ted said, resting his hand on my leg.

Jeremy's outburst made as much sense as Paula's desire to separate the boys. But she had handled a delicate situation with hurtful clumsiness. Her timing and anger were too wounding to comprehend as anything but betrayal, because only a few days earlier, I was catatonic, Ted verged on a nervous breakdown, and Nathaniel turned blue in intensive care. Besides, I envied her freedom to walk away. At moments, we wanted to bail out because it was too much for us, I thought. But we did not have the choice.

∞

How could anyone know what the last four days had been? How can anyone ever know another person's pain? For both Ted and me, who had responded with adrenaline clarity to Nathaniel's birth, collapse came later. On the morning after Nathaniel was born, I had surfaced from the anesthetic of sleep, dopey and lethargic, incapable of movement, vaguely sensing an imperative to get up and then more clearly, the reason: the baby.

I pushed the buttons on the hospital bed and sat for a long time trying to break the sorrow that locked my joints. With intense concentration and sheer will, I activated the muscles to turn my hips and dangle my legs over the bedside, sliding closer to the floor. When my bare feet finally touched, I yearned to tunnel back into the forgetful black hole of sleep.

I regarded the flowers on the windowsill like a botanist, transfixed by the sharply etched vision of ruffled blooms on the pink azalea, the tiny orange grains of pollen dusting the lily's crushable petals, the lanky multitude of cheery daisies. Suddenly, one of the vases teetered as if telekinetically jostled by the intensity of my emotions and fell to the floor, scattering shards of glass.

The crash brought a torrent of tears. When my eyes finally dried, the overwhelming complications of the last twenty-four hours faded into the simple and calming choice: to clean up or not to clean up? Now I knew exactly what to do. I got out of bed, harvested the glass, rescued the splayed flowers, and searched for a new vase, secure in that moment in the knowledge that there would be no turning back. Deliberately, methodically, I put on my socks, Ted's T-shirt, pants, replaced the toothpaste cap on the tube, lifted the tangled hair stuck in the bristles of my hairbrush, and folded my dress. Never had I been so liberated by the little housekeeping chores that need to be done.

When the room was spotless, I checked the clock and wondered about Ted, imagining first a car accident and then the possibility that he had been electrocuted talking on the phone during the thunderstorm, which had happened once to a West Point cadet. Now the whole world suddenly felt unsafe. No, of course not, I thought as I opened my door and gingerly padded down the hall to the elevator: he was sleeping in or playing with Jeremy. Besides, Ted had a musician's sense of time, his own internal metronome.

Half an hour later, Ted limped into the NICU, accompanied by two friends, one of whom had done her medical training at Beth Israel. Inexplicably, I thought again of birthday parties, kids in pointy hats, hands and faces smeared with cake, and had another crying fit, the tears salting up my cheek, until I feared that with all of this crying, I would not have enough fluid to nurse.

"There will be birthday parties," they promised, hugging me. "Absolutely."

Ted lowered himself stiffly into a rocking chair with an expression of defeat and sighed, "Sorry to be late but I couldn't sleep. I kept seeing the doctor's face when Nathaniel was born. I was afraid that Nathaniel might depend on us for the rest of his life. I finally drifted off but woke up in tears this morning and didn't want to disturb you. . . ." His eyes sought our friends.

"I asked if he felt suicidal," our friend, the doctor said.

"Did you?" I asked, my eyes widening.

Ted shook his head.

"You just couldn't get out of bed," I said.

"How did you know?" he asked, surprised.

"Same thing happened to me."

∾

After the incident with the next-door neighbors, I watched for signs of defection and listened for hints of withdrawal. Ted generally wasted little time worrying about the opinions of others except when he wanted to persuade them to his point of view, but he listened carefully as I wrestled with the burgeoning awareness that Nathaniel touched others deeply.

In those first weeks, Nathaniel demonstrated better than any magician's trick—that seeing is always a matter of believing, that the eye, brain, and soul are intimately connected, that vision never was, and never can be, a mechanistic process of recording reality "just as it is." Watching others react to our baby was like having a telescope aimed into the deep space of the human heart.

A period of grace usually accompanies the birth of a child. For a fleeting and sacred whisper of time, joy swaddles a newborn so tightly that those who love the child refuse to see or imagine that he is anything but perfect. Nathaniel, however, looked different. There was no way around it.

The fact that Nathaniel was born with observable imperfections meant that we lost the social anonymity that members of the able-bodied, physically "normal" majority take for granted. People paused, stared, and noticed. It was sobering to realize the degree to which primitive responses to deformity have been civilized but not completely erased. At first, Ted and I floundered, unsure exactly what to do about the lingering looks.

Just as others looked a little longer at us, we stared back at them, and in that process, their protective cloak of social anonymity dissolved too. For a brief but essential moment, their private selves became public. I loved sharing random moments with those who had transcended pain, but hated forced encounters with those who lacked the ability to love the human spirit in whatever ephemeral package that it took. Those for whom the future was a gauntlet of pitfall and disaster dwelled on Nathaniel's problems, while people who had never had their own particular beauty embraced had no faith that anyone would embrace his. It was as if they viewed Nathaniel through the smudged window of their own experience and mistook their reflection for our child.

I was grateful for those who gave positive reactions that required no sophisticated decoding, like the friend who sent such a ferocious welcome letter that we asked her to be Nathaniel's godmother, or Ted's mother, who cradled Nathaniel for nearly her entire visit. In a perverse way, I was even grateful when my OB-GYN nurse burst into tears when she saw Nathaniel for the first time, or my cousin who said of course Nathaniel wouldn't have children of his own. This negativity erased my moments of ambivalence, the times when I lost my confidence that Nathaniel was a miracle, just like any other child. If Nathaniel wanted children, more power to him.

But many reactions were baffling, as when Ted's friend Albert cradled Nathaniel with an expression both protective and pained. Did the pain signal compassion or pity? Was Nathaniel's physical appearance a permanent obstacle or a temporary one? What did these nuances matter if the essential impulse was born of kindness? It was tricky to have lunch with a work acquaintance who seized on the moment to re-establish our connection, bringing thoughtful presents but probing with voyeuristic curiosity. Was she a tragedy-chaser or simply eager to show good will?

The slightest recoil in the face of family, friend, or stranger upset my balance, making me anxious at first about taking Nathaniel outside, but it never crossed my mind or Ted's to hide indoors. Nature brought us close to the sacred, mysterious forces of the universe that we called God, and, besides, it was the end of July, too sultry to sit in a house with no air conditioning. Our first excursions to Walden Pond with my older brother, John, and his family, and later my best friend from college, created a painful sense of dislocation. Resting on the strip of sandy beach rimmed by piney woods, I felt protected by their love and insulated by the turbulent hubbub that little children make, but the fact was that no one could look at Nathaniel without looking twice.

On a bright morning in early August, I took Nathaniel to Jeremy's nursery school a few blocks from our home. He was a week old and I carried him in my arms, his favorite angle of repose.

"Nathaniel is sucking on my finger," I told Jeremy.

"Hey, boo-boo baby!" Jeremy said, making a silly face.

Nathaniel's sucking slowed and his eyes shifted towards Jeremy's face.

"He likes you," I said.

Jeremy beamed with pride. I held his hand, savoring the feeling of his soft doughy fingers resting trustfully within my calluses, ropy veins, and bumpy knuckles. He strode with bravado, clad in red boots and fire hat, minus the sword and shield that were part of the dress-up. Together we scanned the gray pavement of the sidewalk, looking for G for the gas line, S for the sewer line, and W for the water pipes.

As Jeremy stomped on the pipe covers, I hoped that his nursery school classmates might be as charmed as Jeremy had been when he first noticed Nathaniel's differences. Nathaniel had been resting on the middle of our big bed, his pliable legs kinked up, fascinated by the dust particles in the air and oblivious to the kinetic energy around him.

Jeremy had lobbed an orange basketball at Nathaniel—one of those accidental-on-purpose gestures that the experts on sibling rivalry had forecast. Fortunately the ball landed without causing harm. When Jeremy retrieved it, he jammed his face against Nathaniel's and inspected his brother closely for the first time. "Look, MOM!" he screamed with the awe-struck joy of an astronomer who has just sighted a new heavenly body in the sky. "Nathaniel has incredible hands!"

"He does, doesn't he?" I said wryly and hugged him.

At Jeremy's nursery school, the kids clustered outside the front door and immediately clamored to see the new baby.

"He's cute," said one girl. "Can I hold him?"

"Not yet," I said unswaddling Nathaniel from his blanket with trepidation. He opened his eyes as if looking through a fog. His tiny arms folded close to his body. "He was just born."

"What's his name?" she asked.

"Nathaniel," Jeremy said proudly.

"His face is weird," said another girl with disgust.

I was unprepared for my overwhelming desire to smack a child who wore a ruffled dress, had a tumble of red curls, and barely came up to my waist. Jeremy was watching and listening, as was the increasingly nervous teacher. I stalled, uncomfortably aware that improvisation was not my forte, yet compelled to master my anger and say something. You can't lecture to a four-year-old about prejudice. She probably couldn't even pronounce the word. She noticed that his face was different than most babies'. . . okay, it was . . . so what?

"He was born—like that," I fumbled.

"His fingers are stuck together," she said smugly, emphasizing the "stuck" so it rang out like a swear.

"Why, yes they are," I pretended to notice for the first time and held my breath.

"I was born with my fingers separate," she said proudly.

"So was I," I replied, stretching them out one by one.

She leaned over to look at Nathaniel again and declared, "He's cute."

The matter closed, she skipped off to the block area. I dissolved into a corner, giddy with relief that Miss Redhead had so quickly converted and yet solemnly aware how unprepared I was for the changes that my life had taken. Jeremy got a puzzle from the shelf, dumped out the pieces, and methodically assembled them, working on the floor with a boy named Zack.

I stared quietly at Zack. When I first met him, Zack was neither walking, speaking, nor looking at other children, the result of a nameless neurological disorder. Exhausted by the demands of keeping up with an energetic toddler, by balancing family and work and the daily maintenance it all required, I could not imagine the distress and added hardship of a child who had skipped from the rails of normal development. Now I was consumed with angry self-reproach, for having once looked at Zack, compared him to the other children in the tidy classroom, and then judged and pitied him for what he could not do. I would kill anybody who dared regard my baby that way.

I kissed Jeremy on top of his head and on the way out, stopped in the school's office where the summer teacher hunched over the desk.

"Are you OK?" I asked, sensing that she was not.

"My husband just had a heart attack," she blurted out, panic-stricken.

"Where is he?"

"In prison," she replied.

I hugged her, saying I was sorry and then mulling over the sticky invisible web of suffering that connects us all, walked home down the shady side of the streets, showing Nathaniel the Gs, Ss, and Ws.

I am building a soap box racer with my Dad. We are at the stage of gluing, stapling, and painting.

It is really fun to work with wood. The table saw is so loud that it makes my ears ring.

# Chapter Three

ᘜ

# A New Family

August 1990

*I*f illness is another country, then a rare birth defect feels at first like a place of exile from which there will be no return. This sensation of loneliness permeated our first visit to Children's Hospital on a beautiful Saturday morning in August when Nathaniel was two weeks old. Ted pressed anxiously ahead while I trudged behind, fixated on the big sign above the hospital's entrance. The closer I got to the sprawling hybrid of bland modern structures and ornate old ones, the more repellent it became. Unlike most hospitals that housed the sacred violence known as Western medicine, this was the Vatican, a world-renowned tertiary care facility, infested with experts who specialized in the exceptional. Families made pilgrimages to it across oceans, continents, and time zones while we simply battled the

crazy drivers and the ineptly signed roads to traverse
the polluted Charles.

Other families on this holy walk commanded my
suspicions. One child with inert legs pushed his little
wheelchair while an elderly couple gently held hands with
their son, a short shambling man with bottle-bottom
glasses and Down syndrome. Did the kids with no obvious signs have leukemia, tumors, the dreaded cancer? At
the entrance, which was set back from the congested
street, I froze, unwilling to cross this building's threshold and puncture my innocence by discovering the endless ways that human biological development runs amok.
Children's Hospital: the entire building ought to disappear. The juxtaposition of those two simple words con-
tradicted my axiomatic belief that doctors should enter
our lives at the end, not the beginning.

The revolving door whirled us in and we threaded
our way to the Craniofacial Centre, whose remote out-
post in the medical complex confirmed the marginal
world into which we had been thrown. One doctor who
had visited us in the NICU had likened Apert syndrome
to getting killed by a lightning strike because the odds
were about the same: 1 in 100,000.

In the cramped and airless waiting room sat another anxious couple holding a baby who, at first glance,
had an elaborate grown-up hairdo, complete with the
poufs and swoops favored by Hollywood actresses in the
1940s. On closer inspection, the big curls were the result
of an enormous lump ballooning out of her scalp.

"Hi," said Ted. After a congenial silence, he asked.
"What does your daughter have?"

"Dr. Mulliken is injecting something into her scalp.
He wants to create extra skin to use for grafts," answered
the father.

Ted nodded with interest as he drew the father
out, coaxing him to explain the operation in greater

detail while playing peekaboo with the baby. I listened while nursing Nathaniel. His big head required extra support and his mouth-breathing made nursing a long process. He sucked and breathed, taking turns just as predicted.

Ted's warm curiosity came as no surprise. His was a medical family and the fact that Ted did not become a doctor merely confirmed what his family had always known: he didn't quite fit in. His mother had been a nurse, his younger brother, Mat, was a resident at a Boston-area hospital, planning to specialize in rehabilitation medicine, and his sister, Betsy, was a psychiatrist in Washington, D.C.

But Ted was also comfortable with hospitals because he was a veteran, whose pragmatic attitude about fixing body parts reflected the large number of his own that had been broken. Most remarkably, he owed his life in some measure to the wonders of medicine, having survived (just before we met in college) a car crash that nearly broke his neck. As a sports nut who had racked up countless surgeries for knee problems, a broken elbow and collarbone, he approached medicine with a sangfroid that I lacked. On a summer midnight ten years earlier, we had waited in a New York City emergency room for hours with bleeders, gunshot victims, and raving maniacs until Ted was diagnosed with a hernia needing immediate treatment. Ted took the news with equanimity but as soon as they started his IV and wheeled him onto the elevator, I blacked out.

The couple disappeared into an exam room and I prowled around restlessly casing the joint, poking my head through doors. While Ted was changing Nathaniel's diaper, I discovered a strange sight in a nearby office. After a stunned moment, I beckoned to Ted, who came in, carrying the baby high over his shoulder. We stared dumbfounded at hundreds of white plaster casts.

Hands! Hands with more than five fingers; hands with fewer; hands with digits webbed, fused, and dangling; hands shaped like claws, paws, and clubs; hands with gigantic thumbs; hands without any at all. Each hand was utterly unlike its ghostly neighbor, each was sui generis, a one-of-a-kind, wilder than the last. It was if we stumbled into a design workshop and peeked into the brainstorming session which took place before the chief executive decided which model to mass produce. Only a short time ago these hands would have seemed deformed but now that we had landed on the continuum ourselves, this term was grossly offensive. Instead, the hands spoke of the infinite variations of life, the pluralism of genetic recombination, the exuberance of evolution, and the novelties that inspire all biological improvements.

Dr. John Mulliken cleared his throat at the door. He was the craniofacial expert who had visited the NICU the day of Nathaniel's birth and answered our first round of questions. Somewhere in his fifties, Dr. Mulliken was old enough to inspire confidence yet young enough to be in his prime. Beneath the standard white doctor jacket, he had a disarmingly friendly manner. His bright eyes, palpable enthusiasm, and quickness reminded me of an otter.

"Are these yours?" I pointed to the hands. Dr. Mulliken shook his head in a friendly way before ushering us into his shoebox office with a rumbling air conditioner.

"You probably want to see pictures," he smiled with guileless simplicity.

Another man filed in, waved to Dr. Mulliken, glanced at Nathaniel and then more cautiously at us. What was he doing, hanging around this out-of-the-way corner on a Saturday morning? I wondered. Something in his manner suggested a high-class shoe salesman, avid for customers but not too pushy. In contrast to the casually dressed, slightly rumpled Dr. Mulliken, he was suspiciously immaculate in his hand-tailored shirt and silk tie and introduced himself with a dance of hand-shakes and a business card decorated with little Harvard coats of arms. The card read neurosurgery, double degree, M.D., Ph.D.

"Philip is part of the craniofacial team," said Dr. Mulliken. "He'll be working with me."

In the NICU, Dr. Mulliken had explained that Nathaniel would need two operations—the first when he was three months old to create a forehead bone, and the second, when he was eight or ten or fourteen years old, to advance the middle of his face, and of course surgeries to separate his fingers, but this was the first hint that a "team" of doctors was required.

Dr. Mulliken grabbed a hefty notebook from the shelf, flipping it open to sheaves of 8 by 10, black-and-white glossies. The difference between art and science, I thought, can be summed up most succinctly by the headshots that actors carry in their portfolios and doctors have in theirs. The actor plays to the inventive imagination while the physician prohibits every emotion, and leaving no pore hidden, attempts to pare the universe down to its stark, indisputable, factual core. My first reaction was that this kid looked like he was sitting under interrogation lights, while my next was this could be Nathaniel's first cousin.

"Here's the child after the first surgery," said Dr. Mulliken, casually flipping the photographs. "The frontal advancement. That's where we bring the top of the supraorbital rim forward." I glanced at our sleeping infant and then at Ted, whose widening eyes signalled surprise and skeptical disbelief that the child looked "better."

A man with a bow-tie ambled in. "Nalt is part of the team," introduced Dr. Mulliken. "He'll be working with me too."

Nalt smiled, shook hands, and passed out his card which read maxillo-facial surgery, failing to explain where that part of the body was located.

"Do you consider this a successful operation?" Ted asked, his impatience growing as the experts outnumbered us.

"Oh yes," replied Dr. Mulliken. His colleagues held their arms across their chests, nodding in unison.

"Could we see a child with results that you don't consider successful?" Ted asked.

Dr. Mulliken yanked another notebook off the shelf. "Here she is after the first operation, which had to be repeated. Here she is after we did her mid-face advancement. That's where we pull the middle of her face forward. Before. After."

Ted and I gaped at the photos for the simple reason that neither of us had ever seen anything like this juxtaposition. *"Altered"?* They've got to be kidding. Words were not adequate to describe what had happened to this child's face. The transformation was mind-bending in its magnitude. The nose, the cheeks, the upper jaw, which had previously been sunken and submerged, had been pulled forward, so that the entire topography of the face was recast. Yet in a blunt moment of truth, as soon as I saw how much the doctors could actually do, I abruptly realized how little.

"She'll need another mid-face, probably when she's sixteen," Dr. Mulliken said in a breezy voice. "But first, we will pull her jaw forward and straighten that."

As Dr. Mulliken pulled notebook after notebook off the shelf and opened them to the black and white glossies, helpfully, candidly, enthusiastically ticking off the mildness or severity of the syndrome, the timing and nature of the surgeries, his pleasure and displeasure with the results, the truth settled in. At Nathaniel's crib side, Dr. Mulliken had frayed the story. We had been lost in fantasyland, so naïve and gullible to believe that an easy fix existed. Our younger son would have many more than two operations and even when he had them, his syndrome would never be erased, extinguished, or camouflaged. He would always look "different."

When Nathaniel began to fuss, Ted reached over and took him out of my arms to comfort him, swaying back and forth, rocking softly from heel to toe on the worn carpet with resignation. I brooded in silence, arms folded across my leaking breasts, warily scrutinizing these glorified carpenters who seemed interested in Nathaniel for his rarity value. Why did they want to put our sweet baby through grueling operations? To be strapped to the great wheel of conformity? To fit some Procrustean bed? What was wrong with the way he looked anyway?

"What if you didn't operate?" I demanded. "What would happen if we decided to do nothing?"

Dr. Mulliken shifted uncomfortably while his colleagues looked down and stared at the carpet.

"Look, well, feel for yourself. He has no bone where his forehead is. He needs surgery to let his brain grow, to protect his eyes, and maybe improve his breathing," Dr. Mulliken said.

"Protect his eyes?" I asked.

"This bone," he pressed on his own bone underneath the eyebrow. "The supraorbital rim forms a hollow in which the eyeball resides. Right now, Nathaniel's eyes are vulnerable to injury because they are not protected by bony sockets. And his eyelids can't close all the way."

"What happened before this type of surgery was done?" I asked.

"People went blind."

"Do you have any pictures of people who never had the surgery?" I asked, doubting that the Earth spun around the Sun.

Dr. Mulliken hesitated and then scavenged through the desk clutter until he found a worn folder and a slide. "This older man was never treated. He lives at the Fernald School, an institution for the retarded in Waltham. The folks with Apert are not retarded. Just looked that way." He paused, his frank voice softening. "They figured that out because the folks with Apert ended up running the place. I don't know if you really want to see this."

"Ted?" I asked, uncertain how much I could see, how much my squeamish system could handle. He was the only person in the room whose opinion I trusted, but I experienced a prick of guilt, wondering where a struggling, adrenalized father would find the courage to overcome his own tender anguish.

"He *is* right," Ted said, quietly tucking Nathaniel to his chin and holding the cardboard frame up to the overhead light. "You don't want to see it."

Every voice of my being screamed escape but for the sake of the baby nestled in Ted's arms, I stayed in the shoebox room with the refrigerated air and the mumbo-jumbo talking doctors. I quieted my churning emotions into an unnatural calm and stepped into my profession, listening as a journalist, drawing on my training in the scientific method to suspend judgment, hold many possibilities in the air and toss them around before reaching a conclusion.

Nathaniel's medical christening, which newborns with obvious medical problems receive, was a mixed blessing. But what blessing is not mixed? For the next two hours, the team gave a private tutorial, through which Ted and I stumbled and faltered in our efforts to grasp the relationship between bony structure and facial appearance that was second nature to them. Later Ted said that he wished for clay to sculpt what he learned about the skull beneath the skin. Like a blind woman, I stroked the contours of Nathaniel's face, Ted's, and then my own to understand the spatial relationships, the unique proportions, angles, and planes in the face's anatomy.

I reached the limits of what I could absorb and retired to a nearby chair to nurse Nathaniel, knowing that I need not understand everything at once because it would eventually make sense. But Ted pushed on relentlessly, determined to comprehend it all, knowledge giving him the tenuous sense of control that nursing Nathaniel gave to me.

Even half-listening, details that had never been important before became so obvious: skulls are narrower in the front than the back, the eye hides inside the safe dark hollow of bone, the left side of the face faithfully mirrors the right, and the forward planes of the teeth and jaw line up. There is an exquisitely harmonious marriage of form and function in the human body, and every variation in form—particularly in the face and skull and hands—so compromises function that the two are virtually inseparable.

But Ted first absorbed the myriad ramifications better than I. If the bones of Nathaniel's middle ear were fused or too small or out of alignment, hearing would be lost. If the shape of his skull distorted his eye sockets, the precise movements of eight pairs of tiny muscles controlling each eye would be affected and his eyes would not work in tandem, as binocular vision requires. If the nasal passage was pinched, his sense of smell could be out of whack. If the middle of his face was set back, the geometry of the tongue, teeth, and airway would go awry, leaving his mouth so crowded that he would have trouble eating, breathing, sleeping, and speaking. If the skull vault was constricted, then the architecture of the brain could malfunction. If his fingers lacked multiple joints, if his thumb could not meet his other fingertips, he would lack dexterity. Some with Apert syndrome were born deaf while others became hard of hearing. One in five needed tracheostomies, meaning they breathed through an opening in the windpipe.

When these doctors discussed craniofacial conditions—and they sounded like sports fans arguing about favorite teams—Pfeiffer, Treacher-Collins, Pierre-Robin, Crouzon—they agreed that Apert was the hardest to "correct." More than a birth defect, it appeared to be a metabolic disorder, a malfunctioning of genes that govern the growth of the body's bones. For some reason, the scrambled message most affected the extremities, but to one degree or another, none of the skeleton's 206 bones escaped. I had imagined bones to be fixed, solid, and impervious to the passage of time. After all, they held up the body in life and escaped decay in death. But I knew now that my newborn's bones were dynamic reservoirs for the unpredictable randomness at the heart of the universe.

"What can we expect?" I asked solemnly.

"Basically, he will be a typical kid who looks . . . different," Dr. Mulliken said carefully.

This made no sense, I thought. How could Nathaniel possibly be typical after the doctors had just spent two hours explaining that every square inch of his body had endured an insult? Was he trying to mollify us?

"Do you have data that correlates the severity of the syndrome with outcome?" asked Ted, who preferred the clarity of numbers to words.

"There just aren't enough people for studies."

"In your practice, what have you seen?"

"The syndrome is very difficult to predict." He was buying time.

"Any generalizations?" Ted pushed. The air conditioner wheezed as the doctors were momentarily silent, trying to pin down a reasonable probability, a definite maybe.

"Personality," Dr. Mulliken finally affirmed. "A lot depends on the kid's personality."

I looked at our tiny new baby, wondering yet again who he would be.

"After the first operation, what happens?" Ted asked.

"The timing of the midface surgery—it all depends. Some kids need it to help their breathing. Some for psycho-social reasons. The teasing can be rough. So we monitor his growth. Wait and see," said Dr. Mulliken.

"For how long?" Ted asked.

"Until his bones stop growing. For a boy, that is usually somewhere between sixteen and twenty," said Dr. Mulliken.

"So we'll be working with you for the next twenty years?" I asked in dismay.

The team of doctors nodded benignly while Dr. Mulliken, looking sheepishly around said, "Unless I'm retired first."

∞

In a tiny park next to the parking lot, hidden between two grimy buildings, Ted and I slumped on a wooden bench under the shade of a stunted maple tree, and, as we had done so often in the last two weeks, simply held each other. The tears that dried up in front of strangers fell now, making little dots on the blanket in Nathaniel's car-seat.

"You're probably wondering why we are always crying," I said to Nathaniel, who seemed to be watching the sparrows flit for bread crumbs at our feet. He was so tiny, his skin just beginning to dry out from the amniotic bath, the womb still a fresh memory. He had no schedule, except the ecstasy of nursing, the despair of hunger.

"Maybe you'll be an ornithologist," Ted said, for that was what he had wanted to be once.

"Or a gardener," I said, for that was what I had wanted to be once.

Ted and I clasped hands and stared in each other's watery eyes, knowing that we had crossed a boundary and would never go back. In the vibrant purity of the moment came the expansive sensation that everything in the world was irreplaceably precious—the carefully arranged red bricks on the nearby building; the thin lines of gray mortar between each one; the sparrow's slender wing; flat green leaves generously offering themselves to the sun; a thoughtfully placed bench under a resplendent shaft of light; the very molecules of life-sustaining oxygen in the sweet summer air; the wild blue yonder of the infinite sky. For a brief moment, the little park felt like Eden. Everything mattered. Everything had a place and purpose.

Then, imagining taunts, teasing, and ostracism powerful enough to convince an insurance company to authorize surgery, I wept again.

"He won't be an actor," I sniffled.

"You don't know that," Ted replied.

"With his appearance?"

"He might like to be the center of attention," Ted said.

"On stage?"

"Sure. It depends on who he is," Ted said.

Why was I arguing? Acting had never been a profession that I particularly dreamed for any child. But the face was our passport to the world out there and the prospect of prejudice and playground slurs, dreams denied and horizons limited by virtue of something as banal as appearance wrenched my soul. All of the dreams that we had for you, little baby, I thought, we have to dream them over again.

"How will he deal with the stares? The teasing?" I wondered.

"He'll learn," said Ted simply. "We'll help him."

∾

For Ted, who was more romantic dreamer than worrier, the team's tutorial accentuated his isolation, making the syndrome even wilder and more remote than it had seemed before. He wanted a cartographer who had surveyed the territory and plotted its summits, valleys, and outcroppings with contour lines, but none existed so he figured that the next best thing was to locate a fellow traveler who could at least orient us to the terrain.

"Other families will give us an idea what to expect," said Ted, who had no inhibitions about button-holing strangers. In New York City, he had spotted a clocktower one day where he wished to live, rang the doorbell, chatted up the owner, and an hour later rented a room.

"What if it's awful?" I asked. Jeremy's preschool peers had already pushed my natural talents for diplomacy to their limits. Besides, what would these families give us? I wondered. A map was only a seductive fiction. "You Are Here" never really explained how you got there, or, more importantly, where to go next. And, as an expert worrier, I did not need to know the whole truth to prepare a defense against it.

"Then we'll know."

"But I don't want to know right now. Maybe later," I said wearily.

"I do," he snapped. A twenty-page pamphlet had spelled out in accurately gruesome detail all of the things that go wrong with the syndrome but since the relevant facts for Nathaniel as an individual could not be plucked from the aggregate, it sparked more questions for Ted than it answered.

"Then you call."

"Fine," Ted replied, stomping out.

∽

The first woman was out so Ted left a message on the answering machine. When she called back, Ted was out at the neighborhood grocery store getting a half gallon of milk so I talked instead.

"Nora is a great kid," said the Mom, whose voice sounded so happily normal. "She's five, in kindergarten at our local school."

"Do you have any other kids?" I asked, thinking about how trivial the usual sibling rivalry worries seemed now.

"No, she's my one and only."

"How is she, um, doing?" I was uncertain how to phrase this.

"Fine. Sometimes she has a hard time hearing if the teacher talks real quiet but she has friends, loves to swim."

"What about teasing?"

"Sure. Occasionally. I'd say that most of the time, kids just look and don't say anything. A few ask, like, what happened? One kid called her melon head, which was crushing until you realize that every kid gets teased about something. Just a second. Yeah. That was the doorbell."

I tried to recall what Ted wanted to know. "How has your husband been?"

"You mean Nora's dad? When she was born, it was tough. He pretended that it was no big deal, but it was. He really couldn't handle it. We split up when Nora was six months old. Sorry. Please call back. I'd love to talk more."

∽

Ted made the next call and I listened on the speakerphone.

"Tony is a great kid," said the dad. "He's in third grade. He gets winded playing soccer and has a hard time tying his shoes but big deal, you get Velcro. Otherwise, he's doing fine. We also have a three-year-old, Lily. That was tough having another one. I worried about cerebral palsy, seizure disorders, cystic fibrosis. There's a whole floor of kids with cystic fibrosis at Children's."

"You didn't worry about Apert syndrome?"

"Nah. Way too rare."

"How many operations has he had?"

"I forget. Two on his head, four on the hands, one for tonsils. The operations are tough. A lot of the doctors and nurses, even at Children's, don't know anything about Apert syndrome. So you gotta watch them like a hawk. My wife lost her job because she never left Tony's side when he was in the hospital, but now she's studying to be a physician's assistant. Figured that she had learned enough."

∞

Curiosity overcame my reluctance and I made the last call.

"Ruth is two," said her mom. "She's a great kid. I don't really know where to begin. Be prepared to spend a lot of time in the hospital. Ruth has had eighteen operations."

"Eighteen?" Nearly once a month. The kid had been raised in captivity.

"Yeah," she sighed. "Most aren't like that. Maybe I could drop off some stuff. Where do you live?"

"Cambridge."

"Lucky to be so close to the hospital. We're up in Maine. Over two hours each way, but listen, I'm in town tomorrow. NOVA did a show, did you know? I'll bring the video and you can meet Ruth. By the way, Apert kids drool, just so you aren't surprised."

I hung up the phone and sobbed until Mom came running from the kitchen, drying her hands on her apron, panic-stricken. "What is it?" she asked.

"Nathaniel is going to drool," I snuffled into her arms. I thought Ruth's mom meant forever. How could an adult live a normal life and drool? I couldn't imagine.

Next morning, the doorbell rang and four jovial people with pleasant voices clambered up to our apartment—Ruth, her big sister, the father toting a stack of official-looking papers, and the mother, arms freighted down with presents.

"He is so cute," she declared, rushing over to inspect Nathaniel, curled up asleep on the living room couch. "I just love Apert kids. He is breathing quietly. Ruth sounded like a hurricane. They put her on a respirator when she was born. Stayed for weeks. Is he nursing?"

I nodded, stealing a look at Ruth, wondering if this would be Nathaniel in two years. Ted sat at the dining room table with the dad, methodically sorting through a small library of medical papers, while Mom supervised the kids, who climbed into the top bunk and built a fort. Like Ted, she had been eager to meet other families but now she was studying Ruth with that quizzical, intrigued expression that strangers used with Nathaniel. Jeremy, who missed his playmate next door, perked up, including Ruth and her big sister in constructing a fort without a pause.

"We know a lot of kids with Apert," said the mom eagerly. "We figure that there's 2000 in the United States but there's really no way to know for sure. I brought some pictures. Have you met this girl? Her forehead is kind of bumpy. This boy? He was born in Korea and adopted by a Connecticut couple. His fingers still aren't separated. No one brought presents when Ruth was born," she said thrusting gifts in my hand. "People just didn't know what to do."

"Thank you," I said, touched.

"How's your family been?" she asked.

"Very supportive." I said.

"My Dad refused to hold Ruth when she was born. Now you've got to pry the two apart."

"How has your older daughter coped with this?" I glanced over to the bunkbed just to make sure that Jeremy was behaving himself.

"It's taken a big toll. Miriam has gotten lost in the shuffle. She sees a therapist at school. Having a kid like this . . . well . . . you know."

I didn't.

"Ruth, hon. Come here a second and show us your fingers." Ruth came from the bedroom and agreeably let her mother hold her hands. The fingers looked like sausages—puffy, untapered, and without joints.

"What can she do with her hands?" I asked.

"Everything."

That's what the hand surgeon had said. Except for tasks requiring extreme dexterity, like buttoning the tiny button on a shirt collar, people adapted in amazing ways to use whatever they had. He told us about a woman born with "lobster claw," an even more complicated syndactyly than Nathaniel's, who became a concert pianist, which seemed impossible until he emphasized that she had the talent, motivation, and support that came from being born into a family of concert pianists.

"Want to see some more pictures?" I nodded while Ted looked over my shoulder. "This is Ruth at one."

She was adorable, beaming out from a pile of Christmas paper wrapping, but something was off. "Are her eyes OK?"

"No, they were just beginning to prolapse then," she explained. "Pop out."

I tried to suppress a gasp.

"Oh, they didn't come all the way out," said the father. "But the eye-sockets were so shallow that the skull just couldn't hold them in."

Would I sound like this one day? I wondered. He could have been talking about train schedules.

"What happened?" Ted asked.

"We had to do the mid-face surgery."

"That's where they move the middle of the face— the nose, cheekbones, and upper jaw—forward?" I was getting the lingo.

"Right. I've forgotten how many times they have opened Ruth's skull. So many complications. You don't want to know."

Ted did. He jumped right in. "Like what?"

"She had a tracheostomy. One lung collapsed. She got pneumonia and almost died. Her skin grafts failed."

"Just one skin graft, honey," the dad corrected gently.

"You lose track after a while," the mom apologized.

Mom was eavesdropping by the door with a stunned expression indicating that she cared more about this than whether a kid fell off the bunkbed.

"Get all the services that you can. Physical therapy, occupational therapy, speech therapy. By the way, no one has heard of Apert syndrome. People think she has Down syndrome."

We watched the NOVA video until the camera went inside the operating room to show a surgery and then I couldn't turn the TV off fast enough. Ted and I shuffled medical papers until our eyes glazed over. Nathaniel woke up, fussed, nursed, and then went back to sleep, while Mom served lunch, cleared the table, and washed up. When Ruth and her family departed hours after they had arrived, Ted and I flopped on the living room sofa, heads resting on a pillow at each end, legs entwined in the middle, like pretzels.

"Their experience makes the Hindenburg disaster look like a Boy Scout campfire," I said, trying not to sound as discouraged as I felt.

"Why did they tell you everything?" Mom said, slouching in a chair with Jeremy perched on her lap. "Why did they stay so long?"

Ted shook his head while I stared goggle-eyed. This helpful visit was beyond our worst nightmare.

"Is this what we have to look forward to? Eighteen operations over the next two years? Is this going to be us?" I asked, terrified that it would be.

"Not if we have a choice," said Ted, stunned.

What disasters would be ours, I wondered as a fire engine wailed in the distance. A future where Nathaniel had too many operations to remember? Where everything that could go wrong did? Where Ted got fired? Our marriage broke up? Where Jeremy was troubled?

One of the books that I had read during pregnancy likened a second child to adding another passenger to a small sailboat. Everybody in the family had to scoot around and reposition themselves before the wind could fill the sail and push the boat along. Perhaps family was the sailboat that Jeremy had envisioned in his letter to Nathaniel. But Nathaniel, no ordinary second child, could swamp us, no, capsize and drown us all, destroying what he needed most. As Jeremy rushed to the sofa and climbed over legs, gazing elatedly through the screens at the rumbling fire truck, it sank in for the very first time—the brutal power of forces beyond our control.

"A healthy child, that was the only thing I wanted and I refuse to give up on that," I said, fighting back. "His bones may not grow right but he can be healthy in heart and soul. I'll settle for two out of three."

"Nathaniel's bones," said Ted, strategizing quietly. "The operations. All of that will be whatever it is going to be."

"Apert kids," I fumed. "What the hell is an Apert kid?"

Ted looked puzzled.

"He is a kid first, not a syndrome," I declared.

Ted nodded, mustering his own forces, as if saying the words out loud made them true. "Jeremy is a kid first too. Nathaniel's medical problems should not take over his life."

"Or yours," Mom said. "I will come for all the operations. At least, I think I can."

"We need you," Ted said.

I yawned, exhausted. Nathaniel fussed all the time. He napped in two-hour stretches and since only nursing consoled him, my days and nights blurred into a grey continuum. I was so tired that my name and phone number disappeared from memory. One evening, after instructing Jeremy to put on his teeth and brush his pajamas, I spilled into bed fully dressed and conked out under blazing lights. One afternoon when I was pushing the kids down the sidewalk in the double stroller, a car honked and I thought, what a rude driver. Even after the car swung over to the curb, I didn't recognize that it was our own nor that my younger brother, Charlie, was at the wheel.

That afternoon, not long after Ruth and her family departed, I fell asleep on the sofa, waking only when the UPS man rang the doorbell. He had a chirpy grin and many solicitous queries. He had made so many deliveries that Jeremy equated his little brother's syndrome with Christmas, a perspective that helpfully balanced out the letters of condolence that came too. Refreshed by sleep, I sat on the front stoop, sorting through the mail and watching Ted, Mom, Jeremy, and Nathaniel troop back from their excursion to the fire station. When Ted parked the stroller on top of the little green maple helicopters that skittered across the sidewalk, I remembered that

Jeremy, in an angelic mood, had asked if we could look at the wind under the microscope.

"Be gentle with the baby," I reminded Jeremy as he patted Nathaniel a little too firmly.

"He doesn't know anything," Jeremy said.

"You know a lot," Ted grinned.

"Check this out," I announced. "Nathaniel has membership in an order of Catholic saints, thanks to one of Jane's office mates. My grandmother is surprised that we are smiling in our photographs. And another condolence, which I hate."

I passed a letter to Mom. She had stayed so long that she was now getting mail at our address.

"Time to send out birth announcements and tell people we are happy to have Nathaniel here," Ted said.

Jeremy ripped the wrapping paper off another big brother present, this time from my step-relative, who, fifteen years earlier, had a baby also named Nathaniel, who died from a severe birth defect. The coincidences seemed to be accumulating like an endless winter snow. First the intensive care dream, then Nancy's photographs, now this. But what did they mean? In the cool language of science, a coincidence was two events that took place simultaneously, a convergence of statistical probabilities that can be calculated and plotted on a spectrum of likelihood. Some embodied cause and effect and others revealed a suspicious association, but for most, the meaning was a mystery.

One New Age friend drove me crazy when she piously intoned that there were no accidents in the universe. Who was she to deprive the cosmos of its right to be irrational? Her fatalistic line of thinking came dangerously close to the scientists who believed that everything could be explained, that intangibles were merely incomplete data. In the deterministic universe, my friend and the scientist found common ground. Were our choices merely an illusion?

I hated the idea that Nathaniel's syndrome was preordained. It was too neat, too simple, too packaged. Besides, it raised many more questions than it answered. Was everything in life preordained? It was a dangerous act of hubris to read every coincidence as the hand of fate. Mom had glimpsed a stranger on the train to Boston on her way to graduate school, thought to herself, there's a good-looking man, and when Dad turned up at her dorm three weeks later, as her blind date, she thought the omen meant lasting love.

Flushed with excitement, Mom waved her letter in the air and exulted, "I've got Nathaniel's future right here."

Ted looked up. "How did you manage that?"

"My friend did his horoscope," she said.

"We could have checked the newspaper," Ted said.

"Oh no. She's a *Jungian*. Listen, listen up. He *is* a miracle! A Leo with his sun in Jupiter. A big-hearted, strong personality. Loves to be the center of attention. Very sociable and affectionate, with a powerful spiritual sign in Capricorn. Many restrictions. Well, that's to be expected, isn't it? Some of which could be broken down in an upheaval. And listen, I like this: older people will be important in his home life." Mom smiled.

"How did your astrologer ever guess?" I asked, gazing at Nathaniel in the stroller, sucking his thumb, which, by sheer chance, had found its way to his mouth. He had no sense yet of the separateness of his body parts.

"I'll get your horoscope done too." Mom ignored my cynical edge.

"Why not?" I gave in, not knowing exactly what or how to believe any more. Why not read Viking runes, sheep entrails, tarot-cards, and tea leaves? Why not ask psychics and channelers, invoke Jung's synchronicity, and the forces of the collective unconscious? To fuel my own spirits, I needed to imagine the best ahead, to dream the dreams that protect and shelter a child. The flower of hope mattered more than the particular seeds from which it grew.

"He'll be a great kid," Ted said tenderly, pushing the stroller with his foot across the maple helicopters.

"Everybody says so."

"Nothing about a future on stage?" I asked, warmed by the horoscope despite my better judgment.

Mom skimmed the letter and shook her head in puzzlement but Ted caught my eye, grinning.

"A joke," I said. "A joke."

I am good in math. This
year we are learning
    our multiplication facts.
My Favorite is to make
word stories about Nubers.

# Chapter Four

‿

# ℬloodknot

September 1990

*T*he horoscope aside, Mom dwelled on the coincidences of Nathaniel's birth because she was at
the center of a big one. As much as daughters need mothers when a baby is born, so do mothers need daughters.
But my mother especially needed to help because she
wanted to ensure that her past did not become our
family's future.

The year of Nathaniel's birth, my grandmother, for
whom I was named, lived alone, by sheer determination,
in her exquisite house balanced on the incline of the Berkeley hills. She was ninety-four, and age had extracted
its grim tolls. Ganny, as nearly everyone called her, no
longer drove the perfectly maintained Chevy that she
leased from Reggie Jackson's dealership in Oakland,
having reluctantly given up her license after one too

many fender-benders. She was now safely chauffeured by her best friend from childhood, who was ninety-three. She walked with a cane, sometimes a walker, her once perfect posture stolen by time and gravity. She rode the mechanized chair up and down the stairway because her joints throbbed with arthritis, although she rarely complained. Without fail, she dressed immaculately in stockings, pumps, earrings, pearls, and a discreet medallion around her neck so she could beep for help if, God forbid, she fell. Every morning, the local hospital checked that she had not and every evening, one of her three daughters called to talk.

EJ, short for Eleanor Jean, was the oldest daughter and by temperament the calmest. My mother, Julia, was the emotional middle child—the relatives declared that she took after the large-hearted, impulsive, Hawaiian side of the family. Ruthie, the youngest, was a paragon of efficiency, capable of organizing a small country and the only daughter still living in California, so it became her responsibility to help Ganny once a week with balancing her checkbook, grocery shopping, and reminding her that she did not need to give money to telephone solicitors just because they had nice manners.

On one of Ruthie's weekly visits after Nathaniel was born, Ganny signed the monthly check to Pacific Gas and Electric and mentioned that a man had stopped by to fix some equipment.

"I don't remember that the utility scheduled a visit," Ruthie said. "Are you sure that he was with the utility? Did he show any ID?"

"I think so," Ganny replied. "I wasn't going to let him in at first but he was very well dressed."

Ruthie went into high gear and before Ganny could blink, she discovered that Pacific Gas and Electric had not authorized any visits, routine or otherwise, to

Ganny's home. Then she phoned the Berkeley police, who had not heard of any recent burglaries in the neighborhood, but said there was one report of an attempted break-in, and given the thugs who preyed on the elderly, it sure sounded like someone had cased the joint. Until they sent over an officer to get the particulars, better keep a close watch, at least shore up the alarm system because frankly, a ninety-four-year-old lady, alone, in a beautiful house at the end of a cul-de-sac, was a sitting duck.

Within a month, Ganny's peaceful house became a citadel of safety, featuring new locks, non-breakable glass on all of the doors, special motion detector lights ringing the perimeter, and a phone next to each favorite chair. Meanwhile the daughters fretted.

"How could she? Do you think Mother was . . . confused?" Ruthie asked.

"Oh, she's always paid too much attention to what people look like," replied Julia.

The attempted break-in called for new plans. Since Ruthie was going on vacation, EJ offered to stay with Ganny, a visit that passed pleasantly until one night, when Ganny settled on the couch and peered at the TV listings through her reading glasses. With the curtains in the family room drawn over the eucalyptus-scented hills and the burglar alarms set, Ganny clicked on the news, which flashed a picture of a baby girl.

"It must make Jeannie so sad to see a healthy baby," Ganny said. "She must wish that Nathaniel looked like that."

For awhile, they watched the show on the crisis in medical care together, an exposé on why the United States, the richest industrialized nation in the world, rated twenty-third in infant mortality. Then EJ entered the little room which her father had designed for talking privately on the phone and called Julia.

"I get so mad," EJ said.

"Ganny can't help it," Julia said.

"I know, I know," said EJ.

When Ganny saw the baby on TV, she spoke out of empathy, but also experience, for she had given birth to a child whom she wished looked like all of the others. Seventy years earlier, EJ had been born with an incomplete leg.

∾

My aunt was born in 1922. But it wasn't until the 1950s that Ganny's obstetrician—Dr. Frederic Loomis—wrote an account of EJ's birth, with names changed and details altered, which *Reader's Digest* published as a "Drama in Real Life." In the interim, the practice of medicine had been transformed by antibiotics, X-rays, and the polio vaccine, but the story wrestled with the deified role that Dr. Loomis's generation of doctors held.

"To my consternation, I realized that the other foot would never be beside the first one," wrote Ganny's obstetrician, describing how he had just reached in to reposition EJ because she was breech, feet down, head up. "The entire thigh from the hip to the knee was missing and the foot would never reach below the opposite knee. And a baby girl was to suffer this, a curious defect that I had never seen before or have I since.

"There followed the hardest struggle I have ever had with myself. I knew what a dreadful effect it would have upon the unstable nervous system of the mother. I felt sure that the family would impoverish itself in taking the child to every famous orthopedist whose achievements might offer a ray of hope. Most of all, I saw this little girl sitting sadly by herself while other girls laughed and danced and ran and played—and I suddenly real-

ized that there was something that would save every pang
but one, and that thing was in my power to do.

"If only I did not hurry! If I could slow my hand, if
I could make myself delay those few short movements.
It would not be an easy delivery anyway. No one would
ever know. The mother, after the first shock of grief,
would probably be glad that she had lost a child so sadly
handicapped.

"'Don't bring this suffering upon them,'" the
small voice within me said. 'You probably can't get the
baby out in time anyway. Don't hurry.'" He had already noted that one in ten breech babies died during
birth in the 1920s.

"I motioned to the nurse for warm sterile towels—
always ready for me in a breech delivery to wrap around
the baby's body. But this time, the towel was to conceal
that which my eyes alone had seen. The decision was
made. I glanced at the clock. Three of the allotted seven
or eight minutes had already gone. Every eye in the room
was upon me. These nurses had seen me deliver dozens
of breech babies successfully—yes and they had seen me
fail too. Now, they were going to see me fail again. For
the first time in my medical life, I was deliberately dis-
carding what I had been taught was right for something
that I felt sure was better.

"I slipped my hand beneath the towel to feel the
pulsations of the baby's cord, a certain index of its condition. Two or three minutes would be more than enough.
So that I might seem to be doing something, I drew the
baby down a little lower to "splint out" the arms, the
usual next step, and as I did so, the little pink foot on the
good side bobbed out from its protecting towel and
pressed firmly against my hand, the hand into whose
keeping the safety of the mother and baby had been en-
trusted. There was a sudden convulsive movement of the
baby's body, an actual feeling of strength and life.

"It was too much. I couldn't do it. I delivered the baby with her pitiful little leg. I told the family and the next day, with a catch in my voice, I told the mother."

The baby was my aunt. Ganny went through the motions of feeding, diapering, burping her firstborn while all four of the baby's proud grandparents watched her heartache deepen, sinking like the roots of a tree into parched ground. One day, Ganny escaped to a sanitarium amidst the fruit orchards and truck farms on the peninsula south of San Francisco. This was not the baby that Ganny had imagined or wanted and for the rest of her life, she harbored guilt not only for bringing her into the world but for having wished her out. But pressed for details, Ganny remembered few, saying that she ran away, had a nervous breakdown, and that, in her era, "we did not talk about it." But Ganny did talk about the article, sharing it with those she trusted, as a confidence, but also with a sense of vindication that sometimes made others uncomfortable.

∾

In September, when Nathaniel was six weeks old, and summer had taken a right turn into fall, Mom and I talked at the edge of a grass tennis court in Brookline, where her husband, Ferd, was competing in a tournament. Mom had grown up in Berkeley with a racquet in her hand, even had a chance to go pro, and was still a strong enough player to cover the court for Ferd, who moved slowly. Ferd, short for Ferdinand, was eighty-nine and modest about his celebrity on the national "super seniors" circuit, although Mom liked to show off the tasteful collection of gold balls that he had won for his efforts. Next year he would play the ninety-year-olds, one of whom had been Thomas Edison's office boy, and already he was grumbling about the lower caliber of competition.

Ignoring the medic who prowled at the edge of the court, just in case, the eighty- and ninety-year-old players clucked over Nathaniel with good will. Knowing that their days were truly numbered, they treated Nathaniel without the pity or fear that my contemporaries showed: he had what they did not—a whole life ahead.

"A doctor practicing infanticide on the basis of an incompletely developed leg? That's unbelievable," I said to Mom. Times had changed. When I was a child, the newspaper ran a front-page photograph when Senator Ted Kennedy's son skied on a prosthesis. He had lost one of his legs to bone cancer. "Did Aunt EJ really play the harp?"

At the end of the *Reader's Digest* story, Dr. Loomis had written that he lost touch with Ganny after the baby was born and then one Christmas Eve, many years later, while attending a concert, he noticed an angelic young woman play the harp. Only when she limped off the stage to kiss her beaming mother in the audience did he recognize the infant whose life he had nearly taken away.

"Of course not. And Dr. Loomis never lost touch with Ganny. I used to beat him playing doubles at the Berkeley tennis club. He made up the concert scene," Mom said.

Ferd made a perfect drop shot and smiled gleefully. His opponent, unable to run, much less rush the net, shook his head in self-disgust. These athletes were filled with as much combative vitality as the younger tournament players. Although their old bodies had long ago failed them one way or another, they wasted little energy dwelling on the immutable fact that they had pacemakers, cataracts, prosthetic joints, and double-vision.

"What else?" I asked.

"Ganny may have been a sheltered, naïve young woman but her nervous system was not unstable," Mom replied.

"Why does Ganny like the article so much?" I asked.

"The religious message. Ganny believes, as Dr. Loomis stressed, that EJ owed her life to the grace of God."

"Did Ganny's vision of Jesus come after EJ's birth?" I asked.

"No, that was much much later, when we were all grown up. Jesus appeared one day while she was ironing in the basement."

The ordinary setting strengthened the vision's authenticity.

"How old was Eleanor Jean when Ganny went away?"

"Six months maybe."

"How long did Ganny spend in the sanitarium?"

"A week, a month, I have no idea."

"How did my grandfather react?"

"It didn't devastate Pops the way it did Mother. He was practical, very funny, had several patents, but never expected life to be easy. He always said that his job was to prepare us to fly solo in our warplanes."

"What about your grandparents?"

"Both sets lived just a few blocks from our house. They were close friends, met in 1908 just after the Big Quake and the fire destroyed San Francisco. They belonged to the same Monday night book club, took vacations together. That's how Ganny and Pops met in the first place. When Ganny went to the sanitarium, I'm sure they helped out. My father's mother was especially close to EJ, but all of our grandparents were part of our daily lives, sometimes too much. My grandfather walked me to school every morning until I was too embarrassed to be seen with him."

"After Ganny returned home, why did she never forgive herself?" I had guessed that the guilt was embedded in her soul, like barbed wire under the bark of a tree.

"It was a different era," Mom said quietly. "You have craniofacial specialists, a hospital for children, a network of other families, early intervention, computer databases.

In the 1920s and the 1930s, information was harder to get. Ganny spent ten years searching for a doctor who could rebuild EJ's hip and amputate the tiny foot so she could wear a prosthesis. It was a big deal when she finally located a family in Illinois whose child was born with the same thing. And the whole field of prosthetics did not take off until after World War II, when soldiers came home with missing limbs."

Mom sighed. "And Ganny's always been concerned about what others think. You know how she goes on about the neighbor. Her cold showers. The fact that she walks the hills alone and never plays piano for an audience? It has always been important for Ganny to fit in. Besides, those were the days when a young lady did not go outside without wearing a hat and gloves, even in the hottest summer."

The super seniors finished their match and after shaking hands, talked nonstop, passionately replaying each point.

"Why didn't you teach me to play tennis when I was little?" I asked Mom as she walked over to console Ferd. He was sulking after his loss.

"I didn't think you were interested," she said.

"But I wasn't interested because you never showed me how," I answered pointedly.

"Honey, those years were a blur. I was exhausted, a terrible mom. You kids raised yourselves. If I had it to do all over...."

"But you don't," I snapped, suddenly impatient. In Mom's generation, mothering was so much the expected norm that it was taken for granted any fool could do it. My generation paid for child-care, read endless books, and questioned ad nauseum how to do it best. All this information made us more critical but no wiser. Parenting was still the hardest job out there.

"Regret is not easy to live with," said Mom, her face freighted by memory under the crisp fall sun.

∞

In the past, a child's future was glimpsed in dreams, sinuous shadows around a tribal fire, and stellar clusters against a velvet sky. But on the eve of the twenty-first century, science had become such a powerful arbiter of truth that its information shapes our destinies, steering us through the terrors of the unknown. For babies, predictive value is attached to a uterine photograph and pattern of helical molecules inside the nucleus of a cell.

In the wake of EJ's birth, no one asked my grandparents the one question that people inevitably ask us. Did we know? The quick reply was that Nathaniel arrived the old-fashioned way, without the advance warning given by prenatal tests. But that seemingly simple query unleashed a cascade in my mind. Did we know *what?* Did we know who this child would be? What he would bring to our family? What does it mean to know, especially a child's future?

We had had amniocentesis because I was almost thirty-five, the age at which doctors recommend it. In the fifteenth week of pregnancy, the ultrasonographer smeared my belly with warmed grease and in slow, looping arcs, rolled the wand with one hand while punching buttons, zooming the blurred fetus into focus with the other. She pierced the uterine wall with a long needle, extracted a thimbleful of amniotic fluid, and injected it into a small vial that was Federal Expressed to a laboratory in New Mexico. There fetal cells which had, only a day before, been floating in my amniotic fluid grew on nutrient-rich glass dishes. Within a week, the technicians removed a sample and, under a high-powered microscope, scrutinized the cells' chromosomes and saw the usual number, not crossed or damaged.

In my mind, two test results had been possible: good and bad. The bad kind revealed that something was wrong with the baby. I knew intellectually that "something wrong" covered a vast territory. I knew that amnios were crude, illuminating nothing about the hundreds of genes that make up each chromosome but I purposefully avoided embellishing these thoughts with detail. "Something wrong" lacked a distinct form or particular shape, which kept the terrors evoked by the test more manageable.

Although our amnio had a "good" result, two close friends had not been so lucky. Their ultrasonographers peered into the uterine gloom and found something amiss—an organ oversized, a proportion out of whack—which meant that the fetuses would probably not survive birth and if they did, who could say? Our friends both had experienced troubles conceiving, going through temperature charts, infertility work-ups, semen samples, blood drawings, scheduled sex, the monthly wonder "am I, am I not", then by chance surprise both became pregnant. But chance cuts both ways. Just as precipitously as the ecstasy came, it departed as they and their husbands faced an awful, tyrannical choice, having to imagine what they could literally bear and what they could not.

Our friends had faced paralyzing paradoxes. What parent chooses to see a child suffer and what child born on Earth does not? How do we envision a baby with a disability, syndrome, or disease when we have no intimate, personal experience—when we have never lived with nor loved a person with such a condition? What future can we imagine when society has so cruelly excluded those with disabilities in the past? How many parents would risk having a child with a disability if our culture welcomed, valued, and honored every member?

Society embraces the idea that genes have the power to determine our lives. But many lives have not only been handicapped but destroyed by limits wrongly identified as lying within. Dr. Apert, whose manual on child-rearing was beloved by French mothers at the turn of the century, made this tragic mistake. The pediatrician, who lived from 1868-1940, devoted himself to diseases of children, founded the French Society of Eugenics, and actively campaigned to improve the gene pool by eliminating the unfit or degenerate. Like those whose syndrome he named.

Science supposes a world that exists independently of us, but a child is excruciatingly dependent on us. That's why the choices created by tests like the amnio belong to the individuals involved. But none of the prenatal tests that exist now and will exist in the future can give the answers that parents truly need. No test will reveal how love transforms a family. None will indicate how much we, as parents, can bear.

We take risks because loving a child is one of life's greatest rewards. We discover our limits only by reaching that place beyond which we simply cannot go. When faced with pain, we have no idea if our hearts will be forever broken or simply cracked apart so that they can grow bigger. We live with the unsettling knowledge that some of what we most treasure in life are things that we might never choose.

Nathaniel was a thunderbolt from the blue, a wildly improbable, out-of-left-field surprise, the child we wanted and love but never expected, never imagined. Because Nathaniel was our second, we knew that, deep down, it is every child's mandate to reshape a family. We did not know that on Chromosome Number 10, on one of its thousands of genes, the nucleic acid sequence of adenine, guanine, tyrosine, and cytosine had been re-arranged; we *could* not know how little or how much that mutation would matter.

Still Ted and I pondered—as my grandparents surely did, as anyone who suffers does—why the syndrome happened to Nathaniel, why it happened to us, why pain always anchors life's harmonic chords. The insidious, smoky question disturbed Ted's dreams so that he babbled in his sleep. It snaked through my mind when I saw a baby with a small, round head, blissfully asleep in the arms of an unruffled parent in the supermarket. And it finally devastated me on the day that the birth defects researcher rang the doorbell.

"Mommy!" Jeremy cried. "It's a stranger."

A young woman stood on the front porch. Nodding hello with a blank expression on her face, she entered the house and spread her laptop on the dining room table. Jeremy took up residence in my lap. "Can you play with your Legos?" I asked.

He scooted off and I half listened as the researcher explained the protocol. Nathaniel was upstairs napping. Each day, he hewed closer to a routine, his moods shifting less dramatically, the awareness in his eyes growing brighter.

"Did you bring any copies of your studies?" I asked.

She delved into the briefcase and handed over a neat package of academic papers and reprints. Most of the authors came from the Boston University Medical School and many thanked drug companies for financial assistance, a tip-off to the legal fears that prompted the studies in the first place. Of course, a kid like Nathaniel was one reason that every obstetrician in New York City paid over $100,000 a year for malpractice insurance.

"See Mommy!" Jeremy proudly showed me his Lego creation. He had a long attention span for working with the tiny little bricks and had built an intricate wheeled machine, which he maneuvered with great precision.

"Terrific!" I said.

The first questions asked by the birth defects researcher seemed simple and straightforward. When was

Nathaniel born? After how many weeks gestation? What was labor and delivery like? Then, as she moved on to the pregnancy itself, the questions became more difficult. How many hours of sleep had I gotten? How many cups of caffeinated coffee? Decaf? Servings of leafy green vegetables? Nonprescription drugs?

"I took Benadryl for poison ivy," I said while she imperceptibly raised her eyebrows. "That was in the eighth month."

Of course, Benadryl did not give Nathaniel Apert syndrome but the neatly timed eyebrow lift demolished the barrier erected against my rampant guilt. Now I had to put it back up. Marching through the rationale again, I wondered what foolishness made me agree to do this?

The geneticist who came to the NICU when Nathaniel was born had said that Apert syndrome was almost always a random mutation. A compact woman with a scholarly air, she took a quick medical history, noting that no one in our families had the syndrome.

"That is typical. You face no increased risk of having another child with Apert syndrome, nor do any of your brothers or sisters. But Nathaniel does have a 50/50 chance of passing it on to his offspring. The mutation is what we call autosomal dominant. It was probably present in the egg or sperm," she said kindly. "As far as we know, it was not caused by anything that either of you did."

Ted and I had taken "as far as we know" to be a stock phrase that geneticists politely say to overwrought parents because surely we must have done something wrong. Was it the poison ivy? I wondered. Never had the doctor seen such a severe case that he could do so little to treat. In the eighth month, half of my body, bloated belly included, erupted in oozing, suppurating sores. One eye swelled shut. In the queasy expressions on people's face, I saw a reflection of myself. I lived in Aveeno baths, drenched myself in calamine and at night wore mittens to prevent surreptitious scratching. In the middle of this, I had interviewed New York City's Commissioner of Transportation for an article on operations research, a branch of probability theory typically taught to business school students. He had said, half-jokingly, that he once considered planting poison ivy along city highways to deter people from abandoning cars. I had felt like a walking advertisement for creative revenge.

No. Couldn't be that if the mutation took place before the pregnancy was even suspected. How about that transatlantic flight that Ted took right before Nathaniel's conception? A little aluminum sausage bombarded by cosmic rays from deep space? Don't tell me that's really safe. I ransacked my memory because if I knew how it had happened then maybe it would be comprehensible. If it was comprehensible, then maybe I could understand. If I could understand, then maybe these feelings of terror and helplessness would go away.

Could I blame the soybean farmer whose Illinois farm I visited shortly before Nathaniel was conceived, whose combine I drove while researching a magazine story on organic agriculture? What about our bottled water that came from a local spring situated next to a golf course that uses more pesticide than any farmer? Or lead from the solder in pipe joints delivered in poisonous aerosol form in our shower? What about the painting, scraping, and construction work of our youth? The megawatt electricity generating windmills that Ted had built before going to business school? Electromagnetic fields do very weird things to the body's cells. The scientific and technology advances of the last century responsible for making birth safe for both mother and child, the very ones that were saving Nathaniel's life, now seemed insidiously dangerous, maliciously destructive.

The pediatrician who had mentioned the birth defects study hadn't pushed it, in fact, had emphasized that participation was voluntary, that statistically speaking, birth defects are inversely related to economic status of the parents, that three out of every four remain epidemiological mysteries. But as a sucker for advancing the frontiers of science, I knew that one must search even when there is nothing to be found.

The questions wore on. How much exercise did I get? How often did my heartbeat climb above 100 beats per minute? Did I take hot baths? Hot showers? My strength wore down. This Q and A was a mere formality for guilt that had been decided long ago. You've got to blame someone for an imperfect baby.

❧

That night in bed, I asked Ted, "When you think about Apert syndrome, do you think that it was something that I did?"

"No," he said, offended. "Why?"

"I heard your cousin mention my aunt." Everybody had been pruning the family trees, trying to locate the weakest twigs, the strangest branches.

"He's a jerk. Your aunt has nothing to do with Nathaniel. A coincidence. All of the doctors and geneticists have emphasized that."

"The birth defects researcher came today."

"Why did you do that?" he asked. "You've got enough going on."

"I wanted to help," I said. "But she asked me all these questions about the pregnancy, before I got pregnant. The only question that she asked about you was what kind of job you had. The guilt is too much to bear alone."

"It could have been either of us," he sighed. "It could have been nothing. It's lightning. It just happened."

"Why is that so hard to accept?" I asked.

"I don't know. Our brains need reasons, I guess."

∽

My grandmother's guilt lasted a lifetime. Without witnessing how much damage it had done, I would never have been so compelled nor creative in my efforts to banish my own. Out of the blue, sitting by the window on the living room couch nursing Nathaniel, I had a brainstorm and immediately phoned Ted at work.

"I've got it!" I said.

"Got what?"

"Pretend he's adopted!"

"Who?"

"Nathaniel," I said, suddenly wondering if this weird trick would work for Ted as well as it worked for me. I pictured him in his office building, looking out the window across the wharves of Boston harbor to the wind and ocean which refreshed his soul, hearing him try the idea on, like a new hat.

"Imagine that we had a baby who died. At the hospital, someone asked us to take this one. We said yes. We have no idea where Nathaniel came from or how he got here, only that we love him."

"Hmmmm," Ted said. At least, he didn't think this was nuts.

"That way, I don't feel like we failed every time I look at him." Nathaniel stirred. My hand stroked the soft spot on his forehead where the bony plates had not joined, traced the sunken eyebrow ridge.

"Yeah," Ted warmed to the idea. "Yeah. OK."

That simple mind game, which we played only in the first few months of Nathaniel's life, enabled both of us to make peace with the truth, that the particulars of Nathaniel's origins, like all children's, belonged to the archive of questions with no answers.

Sometimes my mom comes into my classroom to talk about our bees. We have three hives. One day my mom had to pick up a package of 1,000 live bees at the Post Office. On the way home, she stopped in my school. We could see the bees buzzing around.

# Chapter Five

❧

# ℬirth Announcements

*September and October 1990*

*T*ed and I made the rounds of doctors' offices, waiting in so many that we teased each other about writing a guidebook to Boston's practitioners. There was the hand surgeon who kept us two hours in a room with no diversions except an anatomical chart of the knee; the orthopedic surgeon with the bedside manner of a motorcycle gang member; the developmental pediatrician who sounded like a cross between Mr. Rogers and an Oxford don; the exacting cardiologist who treated Nathaniel with great dignity and then repeated every test three times because he couldn't find his glasses.

But we didn't chuckle about the time devoured by doctors' appointments nor the dilemmas that it posed. Taking care of Nathaniel's body was more than a full-time job. There were not enough hours in the day for

Ted to track Nathaniel's highs and lows as well as the stock prices of the newspaper, forest product, and computer service companies in which he invested. When the boss urged Ted to take off time, he really meant that Ted could miss some meetings as long as his stock recommendations still made money at the end of the day. Despite a market crash, Ted had done well. So far.

My work was in limbo. Before Nathaniel's birth, I was writing and mediating in small claims court, and in a nod to family tradition, had applied to law school. My North Dakota grandfather, the eldest son of immigrants, had flipped a coin: heads was medicine, tails was law. He started a law firm in Chicago during the Depression which my father and uncle helped to build into a modern giant. Not only had I inherited Dad's parsing clarity, but, much to my own chagrin, I had also absorbed a contingent mode of thinking based on imagining the worst and then defending against it: exactly what lawyers do for a living. But Nathaniel appeared to *my* coin flip, God's not-so-subtle way of saying that the world did not need more lawyers.

I began to shoulder responsibility on the medical front, aware that partnerships flourish or fail because of the limits to what each person can really do. With my scientific bent and journalistic research skills, I immersed myself in the arid terminology to ferret out the twists important to Nathaniel's story. Information was gold. I asked "had they ever" one thing and "what if" the other, seeking the data necessary to clarify the choices that we faced. If the carpals were ossified bilaterally and he had pseudoepiphysis proximally with side to side fusion at the distal phalangeal, then what did that mean for the future of his hands? Beneath the vocabulary lurked a forest of decision trees whose branches had to be followed until they could sustain the weight of no more analysis.

But each part of Nathaniel's body proved epic. One day belonged to the corpus callosum, a structure in the brain that coordinates the neuronal communication between the left and right hemispheres. Horses lack a corpus callosum, as do some people with Apert syndrome. No one knows what it means for a person *not* to have one. For equestrians, it means that they must mount from one side because the horse's memory for left and right are not the same. We celebrated when the CAT scan, necessary for the first cranial surgery, showed that Nathaniel had one.

Another momentous day was a diagnostic double-header, a two-for-one sedation, to find out if Nathaniel was deaf or would need open heart surgery. But since it was also my first big trip to Children's without Ted, I was happy to have my younger brother, Charlie, come along. I had a special love for Charlie. As an unseen baby in my mother's belly, he was my first memory and then later, an ally in the sibling rivalry dominated by our older brother. He was the first recipient of my nurturing impulses, which, as a big sister, I felt intensely, imagining that I bore sole responsibility for teaching Charlie English. "Hamburger. Not Hamner!" I corrected, despairing that he would ever communicate. It turned out that Charlie preferred to read, having taught himself at the age of four with the baseball box scores in the *Chicago Tribune*. Now, he was thirty-one years old, six feet tall with stooped shoulders, a Cubs fan who could, in a pinch, be persuaded to root for the equally haunted Red Sox, depending on his girlfriend. She had just moved to Boston for a master's degree and Charlie, who advised arts organizations on business matters in New York City, was debating whether to follow.

"Are you serious about Trish?" I asked as we sat in the soundproof booth at Children's Hospital while Nathaniel's hearing got checked.

"I'm too serious," Charlie joked.

"You know what I mean."

"The M-word?" he asked, momentarily unnerved by the audiologist who had halted her recording of Nathaniel's brain wave activity to lunge out of the booth and place the earphones snugly back over his ears. Nathaniel was also sporting a Medusa's head of electrodes glued to his skull. But he snored away, blissfully unaware of his hair-do, having been dosed with chloral hydrate, which was also the sedation of choice used by apartment burglars. I nodded.

"Trish doesn't *really* like music," Charlie said. His own headphones hung around his neck, emitting the antiphonal murmur of a Madagascar musician who played zydeco. Or was it Cape Verdean jazz? Besides baseball, music was Charlie's other obsession. After Nathaniel's birth, when most people brought food, Charlie delivered sonic therapy—gospel and spirituals.

"So? Ted doesn't *really* like to read books." I devoured the printed word in whatever —fiction, non-fiction, cereal box labels— while Ted dined on *Barron's,* the *Wall Street Journal,* and *Businessweek.*

"Why are you so cavalier?" he asked. "You panicked before you got married."

It was true. I had been immobilized by terror. Ted and I believed, as did family and friends, that we had the ingredients to make an enduring marriage, but how could we have the ingredients when there existed no recipe? What did either of us know about marriage when we had only witnessed ones that self-destructed? What gave us the hubris to expect success when half of all couples failed?

"Are you afraid of marriage or wondering if she is the right one?" I asked, suspecting that my brother's ghost-demons were similar to mine.

"We're just . . . different." Charlie shrugged.

I remembered echoing my brother's words nearly verbatim, waving the flag of "different" for the unspeakable fears evoked by the thought of merging two lives together. Since Nathaniel's birth, however, I had questioned why different was always the villain, or why, for that matter, irreconcilable differences became grounds for divorce when every well-matched couple had freightcars of them. The paradox of intimacy was that no two people inhabited the exact same world. Ted was a man. I was a woman. He was from New York. I was from Chicago. He loved the ocean. I loved the land. Numbers were his strength. Words were mine. He was frank. I was diplomatic. He was spontaneous. I deliberated. He slept through earthquakes. I woke at whispers.

"So?" I asked gently.

Charlie looked confused, but there the conversation ended as the audiologist left her booth for the last time to say that the test was over. Then she launched into an explanation of decibel thresholds, the structure of the outer, middle, and inner ear, bone conduction, the aural nerve, eardrums, fluid-build-up, fluctuating hearing losses, silastic ventilation tubes, and the reliability of the audiological brain stem response test. By the time Charlie tromped off to catch the subway and I loaded a whimpering Nathaniel into the car seat, taking care to pillow his head into a position where he could breathe, I was too overwhelmed to think.

As the traffic inched along, I chattered because the sound of my voice soothed and calmed Nathaniel.

"That's Beth Israel where you were born and that's Fenway where the Red Sox play," I said.

But Nathaniel was hungry and his moans quickly escalated to full-fledged cries. I tried to slow the pace of his cries with a lilting rhythm and a high-pitched voice.

"They haven't won the World Series since 1918. That's when they traded Babe Ruth to the New York Yankees."

Nathaniel's cries had become urgent sirens. I longed to clasp his tiny shaking body to my breast.

"Hey there, little love, Babe Ruth made the home run into baseball's ultimate weapon," I said. Nathaniel hated the car seat so much I wished that the chloral hydrate was not wearing off. I turned silent, marveling that I had absorbed so many facts from Charlie that I could not say "home" without thinking plate. A truck driver cut me off.

"Asshole," I barked and then said in a pleasant singsong to Nathaniel, "He was a typical Massachusetts driver, sweetheart. Hang in there."

Nathaniel's wails sputtered, his breathing slowed, and his intermittent cries became less forceful. It took an eternity to get onto the entrance ramp for the highway but by the time I merged into the whizzing cars, Nathaniel was asleep and my eyes clouded with tears. "Oh shit, I can't see," I said, panicking that this little grenade of grief had so inconveniently exploded at high speed. The last one had come in the safety of the basement, shifting laundry to the dryer.

Back home, Paula waited on the front stoop with a potted plant and a birthday card. Although Jeremy and Ben still had a moratorium on playing together, Paula and I had gone out to a restaurant after her vacation and had a polite conversation. She had brought over a beautiful book of poems with an apologetic note but things still weren't right.

"How did it go today?" Paula asked pleasantly. She was trying. The least that I could do was lighten up.

"Great! Nathaniel's not deaf and doesn't need open heart surgery!" I said, thinking that this news was my best birthday present. The cardiologist believed that the little holes in Nathaniel's heart would close by themselves and the audiologist said that his hearing problems could be solved by putting tubes in his eardrums.

But when Paula smiled tightly and backed off, I realized that there had been an edgy tone to my voice, an intent to drill it home that, for me, a good day got measured on a new scale.

∾

What is in a face? I know one mother who believed that her little princess was so incredibly beautiful that when strangers didn't stop in the street, she was offended. Like countless others, she became aware of this temporary insanity years later as she leafed through the photo album. "That bald, pudgy, goggle-eyed thing? What came over me?" But I did not begin to grasp the power of a baby's face until Nathaniel joined our family.

In October, Nathaniel was nearly three months old, a social baby now, making eye contact, smiling and vocalizing, fascinated by faces himself. Although the control of his gaze was not strong and his eyes did not always track together, he was beginning to sense that he was separate from us and beginning to make his preferences known. He responded to Jeremy with particular joy—as if to say, *he's a child, like me!*

Nancy Burson flew up from New York City to take Nathaniel's picture. She erected her umbrella lights, spread a sheet over our big bed, and used a cheap camera that made fuzzy, dream-like images. "He's adorable," Nancy said, as Nathaniel flashed his toothless grin.

Nathaniel was Nancy's first subject for a series of photographs of children with craniofacial conditions and progeria, an even more rare condition of premature aging and death. Ted worried that he might not like the photos, or worse, that Nathaniel might not like them when he grew up. While harboring Ted's fear that Nancy might expose our child to public judgment, I snapped our own camera incessantly and pored over each photo, searching for the one that captured Nathaniel at his "best." But what single image ever manages to do that? My parents prized one of me, age nine, rolling on a log in a clear, cold Canadian lake. Where they saw youthful exuberant energy, I saw a gawky, unpoised tomboy whose hair had been cut by my brothers' barber and, during my self-conscious teenage years, I could not abide it.

The search for photographs and sensitivity to judgment was shaped by the reality that Nathaniel faced more poignantly, more bittersweetly, than most. For human beings who rely on vision for 70 percent of the information about the world out there, nothing is richer, nothing exerts more power and fascination than a face. Some believe that an infant's first experiences with the proportion and symmetry of the face, the baby's perception of a coherent unity from its individual parts, build the aesthetic foundation for what the adult will consider beautiful. From static yet ever-changing features, the face conveys identity, intention, and emotion. Studies show that in the first five seconds of meeting a person, we make a decision about his character and moral nature based on how we see his face.

It was a chicken-and-egg question: do we like those whom we find attractive or find attractive those whom we like? The particular answer made no difference to me as long as Nathaniel received the fussing, crazy ogling, besotted attention that babies need. When the birth announcements—including a letter of welcome and a photo of Nathaniel in his baby-blue suit—finally got mailed out, the condolences stopped.

But Nancy had greater ambitions, aiming at an audience wider than our friends and family. The timing of her project and Nathaniel's birth seemed an unmistakable shove of fate. When we had first met five years earlier, Nancy was the last expert I interviewed for a magazine article on how we see the human face. The others had been scientists, who devoted careers to the nuances of emotional expression, the sequence of development in visual discrimination, and the neurological intricacies of facial memory. *People* magazine had recently published Nancy's photo of a jowly, wrinkled Princess Diana, which had been created by aging software that Nancy and her husband, David Kramlich, had pioneered. (They had also originated aging software used by the FBI to locate missing children.)

Nancy lived and worked in one of those New York City buildings whose entrance was depressingly smeared with graffiti and saturated with urine, whose creaky, dimly lit elevator gave no promise of safely reaching its destination. So when Nancy had opened the door to her loft, I had been pleased to stumble on such a beautiful oasis, and leave the ugly world behind. Nancy curled on the couch as I introduced myself and explained my odyssey with faces. For scientists whose professional standing depended on accuracy, this was often a tricky moment in which I had to establish my credentials and prove that I would not commit the embarrassing crime of misrepresentation, but it soon became clear that Nancy was listening on more ethereal wavelengths.

The faces assignment had grown out of another unwieldy story on vision, about scientists who probed neurons, studied illusions, and built machines to detect patterns of light in their efforts to unravel the intimate and seamless association of mind and eye.

"What did they find?" Nancy pressed.

I wasn't sure if she would be interested to know the strange little scientific findings that fueled my own sense of wonder: frogs starve if the bugs around them are not moving; we do not experience flickering lights even though we blink every three seconds to keep the corneas wet; there are people with brain disorders who recognize a clarinet upright but fail to recognize it *up-*

*side down;* and kittens raised from birth in an environment devoid of all horizontal lines grow up literally without the neurons that detect horizontal lines.

Nancy was not bored; rather she treated the information the way that engineers handle nuts and bolts, as useful and integral to her creative designs. When she asked with the same intensity about faces, I took it as encouragement and rambled on—the mere hint of a frown on a mother's face thwarts a hesitant child's choice in a fearful situation; the memory for faces is so durable that most of us recognize high school classmates fifty years after graduation; one scientist identified the forty muscles involved in the creation of facial expressions and then proceeded to learn how to control each one; psychopaths, poker-players, and charismatic leaders are experts at squelching emotion before it plays across the face.

Without much ado, Nancy moved to her work table where her portfolio was spread out and asked, "What do you see?"

The black and white head shots were so ordinary that I shrugged, noncommittally, trying to conceal my disappointment.

She had a look of mischief. "They're composites."

Now it was my turn to listen. Nancy's work originated riding the New York City subways where people-watching was the ultimate entertainment, where an astounding variety of faces could be seen for a token. Propelled by a vision of a machine where you could watch your own face age, she had hounded the computer graphics engineers for ten years until advances in technology finally made her dream come true. The artistic bonus was software to merge two or more faces, allowing her to create a believable composite.

What made these ordinary faces arresting were the ideas that they embodied. For "Mankind," Nancy had mixed features of three different races to reflect the correct percentages in the world's population. But my favorite was the "Beauty" Composites. For one face, Nancy had merged five famous movie stars of the 1950s and for the other she had used five stars of the 1980s and then juxtaposed them side by side to illustrate the fickle and iconic notion of beauty in our culture.

The face was the nexus between Nancy's art and my science, the beginning of friendship. When Nancy asked me to write the introduction to her collection of composites, I took the "Beauty" Composites as payment. Like Doc Edgerton and Louis Daguerre, Nancy strove to make visible something that had always been there but that we had lacked the means to see before.

When I was pregnant with Nathaniel, Nancy had a show in Boston at the Massachusetts Institute of Technology and we toured the gallery together, looking at images inspired by her fears during pregnancy and her desire for a child who accepted those with visible and obvious differences. Afterwards confessing that I did not like her new faces, that the composites transformed by birth defects and disease actually disturbed me, she hooted with laughter.

"I think that the images are beautiful," she said.

"You do?"

"All faces are beautiful to me, no matter what," she nodded, aware of how few shared her opinion.

"All faces?" Could I say that? I wondered and then added, "But that's because you see the spirit of the people you create. You don't just see the physiognomy."

Nancy paused. "We were testing a portable portrait machine when a man came by and wanted a picture of his daughter. She was in a wheelchair, bent up, I think with cerebral palsy. A crowd gathered to watch. I combed her matted hair, reshooting until I got the best shot. She lit up. I was watching her father's face. He was oblivious to the crowd. He only looked at her and it was with such love. In his eyes, she was the most beautiful person on Earth. Yes. I wish I had a copy of that image."

Could I really see beauty in every face? Did it require Nancy's unique vision? Or simply a different image of love? Could I get past the barriers of my own fears and prejudices? Was beauty entirely a matter of the heart wholly independent of flesh and bones? If I had had this daughter could I have looked at her with such transcendent love that it changed the way that others saw her?

From the moment Nathaniel was born, Ted and I had no choice but discover our own answers. Ted, who did not embarrass easily, believed that there was no substitute to jumping right in and learning on the job. I agreed, but being more reserved, resented the public floundering.

"There was a woman in the park today," I told Ted at night after the kids were asleep. "And she asked, 'Will he be all right?' What would you say if I asked you, 'Will you be all right?' What the hell does 'all right' mean? Does she mean will Nathaniel be a whole human being who leads a rich and complicated life? Yes. If we and the rest of the world don't cripple him by treating him as something less."

"What did you tell her?" Ted asked.

"I said 'He'll be fine, thank you.'"

Words, like photographs and mirrors, offered a distorted reflection but they were the only medium available at first to represent our baby to the world out there. There was no label, common language, or shorthand with the right shades of meaning that I could offer to strangers. The term "Apert syndrome" was known only to a tiny handful of specialists. "Birth defect" was too judgmental for a baby who was, in our eyes, perfectly fine. "Abnormal" implied a comparison, deviance, and freakish perversity that had nothing to do with the innocence of a newborn. If forced, I simply articulated Nathaniel's condition the way I saw it—tall head, mitten fingers, webbed toes—but often I settled for defensive silence, waiting to see what would happen.

Yet, I floundered far less than many newcomers to the universe of facial difference. I knew that science and art started from the same place, took off in opposite directions only to meet up again. In the Renaissance, scientists worked alone and artists worked in groups while now artists toiled in isolation and scientists pooled their efforts. But by the sheer act of looking where no one had looked before and in a novel way, science and art changed the way that we saw nature and our place in it.

Without ever guessing how useful it would be, I had done my homework and was well-schooled in the insidious ways that pre-existing ideas determine what we see. The history of science was littered with cautionary tales of experts blinded by their own convictions, "objective" facts that merely confirmed the prejudices of the day. Clever Hans was but one example. He was a horse who lived in Berlin in the first years of the twentieth century, able to tell time, identify various colors, solve calculus problems, and answer questions about geography and politics by pawing with his foot or shaking his head. After careful test and examination, leading scientists pronounced Hans not merely clever but brilliant. But the truth which came out much later proved even more intriguing. Clever Hans was ignorant of math but an expert at reading his interrogator's body language, the barely perceptible tension and relaxation of muscles acknowledging when he gave the correct answer.

Even more bizarre than a horse doing calculus was what scientists believed in the nineteenth century about the face and skull. In the early 1800s, phrenologists held sway, arguing that temperament, character traits, even memory and imagination produced certain formations on the cranium, brow, and facial features. They felt the bumps on people's heads and divined what their personalities were like.

When the first human skull fossils were discovered in the 1850s, and the static concept of God-created species was replaced by the idea of evolution, the pseudo-science of craniometry became popular. With calipers and pincers, craniometricians measured brains and skulls and then classified and ranked people on the basis of anatomy. Not suprisingly, their "findings" mirrored the social hierarchies of the era. Smarter, wealthier European men supposedly had "bigger" brains than women and poor, non-European men. From there, Francis Galton, a British biologist who launched the fields of eugenics and medical statistics, made the short leap of reason that found tragic resonance in Nazi Germany fifty years later. A better, more intelligent race of man could and should be created through selective breeding, he argued.

I had always loved science because it was objective, because it described a world that existed separately from us and our feelings; its labels ordered the mess and its theories circumscribed terror within rational boundaries. In college, I had fallen in love with the microscope because it confirmed what my imagination already knew, that nature's secret life was anything but stale, dry, and musty. In my dreams, giant proteolytic enzymes danced like Shiva, cell membranes opened and closed like secret doors, and bacteria formed deep and long-lasting symbiotic partnerships. Science poached into the realm of imagination where appearances had little to do with reality, where the counterintuitive actually did happen!

But love made objectivity absurd. I realized that when Ted and I took the leap into marriage, and then again when Jeremy was born. The ferocity of a mother's bond illuminated Nathaniel's beauty instantly but I had no idea if the beauty in other children would be as readily accessible to me. I suspected—to paraphrase

Macbeth—that there was an art to finding the heart's construction in the face. When Nathaniel was four weeks old, we shared a waiting room at Children's with a mom and her five-year-old boy with another syndrome. At first, I regarded the boy nervously, then just looked in a peaceful way. He had no chin bone and one skewed eye with the skin bunched over it and his lips on one side were twisted, but in the short time required to decipher this, I felt the kid's spirit, elated to see *him*, not the birth defect.

The world would be a very different place if everyone could make this important distinction, especially young children who have a tendency to blurt out what adults have learned to stifle. But millions of years of evolution prepared the brain to discriminate, to distinguish between self and other, friend and foe, kin and outsider. The eyes focus irresistibly on the face because it is a powerful circle of meaning, where life-and-death clues to identity and intention converge. Neurologists have discovered that this information is so essential to survival that there is a cluster of brain cells, dedicated to deciphering, remembering, and reading the face. In the absurdly short space of a lifetime, how could I reprogram all of that?

It was at Jeremy's YMCA swimming class, five weeks after Nathaniel was born, that an epiphany occurred.

"Do I have to wear the bathing cap?" Jeremy asked in the basement locker room as he shinnied up a pole.

"Yes. And take a shower too. Get down, little monkey," I replied.

"Why?" He was at that stage where conversation was like a string of beads, alternating why-because-why-because.

"Because it's time."

"No, why do I have to wear a cap?"

"Your hair clogs the filter."

"What's a filter?"

"It's like . . . a spaghetti strainer. It lets water go out but not the hair. Come on, Jay."

He patted Nathaniel, who was five weeks old, and headed off to the shower. I leaned against a metal locker that banged shut with a hollow sound and began to nurse Nathaniel, my mind idly blank until, across the stuffy room, I overheard a little boy ask his mom:

"Why does that baby have a big head?"

The room shrank. What should I do?

"He has hydrocephalus. Like your cousin," she replied.

He nodded, satisfied. I wanted to hug the mother and child for their matter-of-factness but saved the embrace for Jeremy, who returned at the end of class, a shivering package of energy. He dressed himself and tried to tie his own shoes but could not quite manage the last step of the intricate motions. As I bent over his laces, a voice hissed, "That baby looks like a space alien."

My happiness unraveled in a frantic rush of questions as I looked into the grimacing face of a nearby five-year-old. Had Jeremy heard? Apparently not. He was absorbed in making a bow. I waited, hoping, praying that the second mother would reassure her son as proficiently as the first had done. But from the embarrassed blush on this mother's face, I sensed that she didn't have a clue how to proceed and, worse, that she shared her child's opinion. The mother cast her eyes uncomfortably at the floor, saying nothing. The boy shrank back, his fears confirmed. And now I so trembled with rage that I did not trust myself to say anything at all. I double-knotted Jeremy's shoes, clutched Nathaniel, sped out of the locker room, and, by the time I was halfway up the steep stairs, had my lecture prepared.

Just imagine what had happened to us: Doctors greeted our child's birth with silence. Specialists inspected our newborn, cataloging his deficits instead of his gifts. When our baby was still a newborn, we got a twenty-page pamphlet that spelled out, in small print, all the things that might go wrong.

Your precious little twerp will suffer pain and trauma. That is life's only guarantee. Maybe he will contract brain cancer, get hit by a bus, or become schizophrenic. And maybe he will be lucky and only suffer from high cholesterol and arthritis. His current able-bodied state is as temporary as the illusion that he is perfect. The difference between your child and mine is that Nathaniel was born with his trauma. We will not have to wait around to discover it.

The storm of rage passed somewhere in the parking lot. As I jabbed the key in the car's ignition, I castigated myself for staying silent but then wondered what could I have possibly said? What did hydrocephalus mean to a kindergartener anyway?

Slowly, the realization dawned that the words themselves had little to do with the ease, comfort, and acceptance that the first locker room mom communicated. Whatever got said would never be as powerful as the way that it was said. The secret to handling the inevitable fear and fascination of outsiders lay in the subtler cues— the ones that Clever Hans read so well, the ones that can be summoned but not faked—body language, tone of voice, a positive attitude.

After that, I followed Ted's lead and practiced a little oblivion in public. In Cambridge, with its traditions of Yankee tolerance and nonconformity, this proved easier than imagined. I took Jeremy and Nathaniel on the bus to the Cambridge Common playground, a popular preschool destination outside Harvard Square, where I forced myself to pay no attention to the double-takes and steamed ahead with defiant delight in two little kids.

The last time I had done something like this was in my early twenties, when to support myself as a struggling writer, I joined the New York City carpenter's union. As

the first woman on a job site with hundreds of men, I was—
for six months—a stop-and-stare oddity. I took initiatives
to defuse tension before it built up and fought back when
it got out of hand and in a short time, my oddity disappeared because I did not behave oddly. But being "the only
one" proved lonely and in the end, the construction skills
I acquired had less to do with laying floors than building
a sense of self on my own foundation.

"Mommy, look!" Jeremy was wobbling by on a pair
of stilts that he had found. I grinned, amazed at his physical gifts and wondered momentarily how Nathaniel
would hang from monkey bars if his fingers never curled.
Right now, he was still trying to get his thumb into this
mouth. I sighed, overwhelmed by a future that was too
big to imagine.

"Hi," said one playground mother. "I saw your baby.
My twins were premature. One still has special needs."
She pointed to her perfect-looking toddler whose drib-
bling pebbles clinked on the bottom of the red tube slide.
"What does your little guy have?"

Happy to be asked in such a friendly disarming way,
I told her.

"Must be rare. I've never heard of it. But you'll do
just great. Won't you, cutie?"

The stranger traced the contours of Nathaniel's
hand, which looked quite suddenly like the state of Michigan, saying, "God bless him, he's a gift."

We went skating on the pond at our house. I went skating with my cousin who came for a visit. A shovel, a shoe, and a Tennis ball were frozen into the ice. When we played hockey we did not go close to them.

# Chapter Six

⸙

# Three Months

*October 1990*

*H*ow do you describe the tang of fear? How do you explain that once you recognize all of the things that can go wrong, you don't immediately forget them? Is it possible to convey what it's like to kiss your baby good-bye, knowing that he will have a new face the next time that you see him? Everyone warned us that the first operation would be difficult but just as adults confuse a child's innocence with vulnerability, so we had confused this knowledge with protection.

Three days before Nathaniel's first surgery, when the sugar maple in front of our house flamed scarlet and Halloween pumpkins jeered from the neighborhood's front porches, the countdown got rocky. Ted stayed home with Nathaniel while I took Jeremy and a rented breast pump to our college reunion in Western Massachusetts.

There I dodged the inevitable question: "What's new?" The last three months defied synopsis.

When I returned that evening, Ted looked like a zombie. Nathaniel had cried non-stop for twelve hours. Ted shot out the door for a walk around the block, returning an hour later in a black and white police cruiser.

"What happened?" I asked Ted as he waved good-bye to the officer.

"I got mugged. I was on my way back home from buying eggs and stopped to admire the pottery in the window of that shop, you know the one that no one goes in? In the reflection of the glass, I saw two guys wearing hooded sweatshirts. One tried to grab my jacket but he couldn't get a grip. I spun, I didn't even think, and threw the carton of eggs in his face. Then I ran. A block away, I turned around to look. They were gone. I flagged the cruiser, and for the next forty-five minutes, we drove through the neighborhood."

Only the broken shells remained.

Surgery minus two days. When Mom arrived to hold down the fort, she departed first for the supermarket to stock up on Comet, Windex, and laundry detergent. Then she went over her clothes trying to find the right outfit because there was no better preparation for the hospital than dressing for the occasion.

I dreamt that our family was strolling down the West Side of Manhattan, next to the Hudson River, when the sunny promenade came to an abrupt end. Jeremy ran to the flimsy barrier. I grabbed him before he plummeted down the sheer precipice. Where did the path go? I saw only a ladder and knew that we had to climb down, a prospect that was vertiginously terrifying. Ted went first, and I thought, others have clearly gone this way before, one rung at a time.

On surgery minus one day, the destination was Pre-op, an airy, toy-filled space, adjacent to the official Pa-

tient Entertainment Center where a guitarist sang to a
packed audience of the young, the chemo-bald, and the
restless. The deliberately cheery ambiance annoyed me.

The Pre-op receptionist apparently disapproved of
smiling. She handed out a Dickensian stack of insurance
and consent forms to read, fill out, and sign. In a quick
translation of legalese, the hospital wanted to know: Who
was going to foot the humongous bill? Can our twenty-
five-year-old sleep-deprived medical students practice on
your kid? Do you understand that if something goes
wrong, it is not our fault? (By the way, we are required
by law to inform you that absolutely anything and everything can go wrong every single step of the way.)
Ready to throw the dice? Are you crazy yet? After signing my name several times, I disapproved of smiling too.

The hospital operated on Medical Standard Time,
which bore no relation to the transit of the sun, and I
reset my internal clock accordingly. Short bursts of activity punctuated interminable stretches of waiting. Time
passed faster in gridlock or maybe in counting grains of
pollen on a bee's hind leg.

A voice shouted "Nathaniel" and a nurse whisked
us down the corridor to a cubbyhole labeled "Hematol-
ogy," where it was Nathaniel's turn to part with blood.
If grown-up veins look like garden hoses, then infant
veins resemble ant tunnels. When Ted's brother Mat
was in med school, he avoided—if possible—drawing
blood from infants because it was like dousing, best left
to those gifted with the touch. A plump woman confi-
dently probed Nathaniel's pale arms with well-practiced
fingertips and wrapped a rubber band around his bicep.
In a flash, Nathaniel howled and she smiled: success on
the first stab.

Back in the waiting area, kids in Mickey Mouse
johnnys played Nintendo while waiting to be called for
day surgery. They would be in and out in a matter of

hours while Nathaniel would stay for a week, which, in the era of managed health care, spoke volumes about the seriousness of the operation.

"Nathaniel!"

Again a nurse whisked us down the corridor to a cramped office where the anesthesiology resident, a woman with a Texas accent, listened to Nathaniel's chest with her stethoscope.

"I don't think he's ready for surgery tomorrow," she drawled. "Not with all of this congestion."

I blanched. "He always sounds like that."

"Just a minute. Let me call our head anesthesiologist."

The head anesthesiologist beamed like a flashlight. Unlike the resident, he knew a lot about Apert syndrome, but I was beginning to understand what Tony's dad meant, that even at Children's Hospital, Nathaniel was a rare bird. Maybe I should make things simple and assume that no one knew anything.

"He's juicy," he said planting his stethoscope on Nathaniel's chest. "But that's typical of this syndrome."

The resident shrugged. "We tend to be conservative. It's our job, after all, to keep him alive on the table."

Once again, we retreated to the waiting area, where by now the guitarist, the audience, and the Nintendo players had vanished. I wondered if Mom had found the fabric store to buy the black felt that Jeremy needed for his Halloween costume, although he still had not decided if he was going to be a witch or a warrior. He was at the age where either would be fine. Mom hated driving in Boston but then only Israelis felt at ease in a city where a one-way street sign was viewed as a suggestion. I tried to ascertain if the long-suffering receptionist lacked the facial nerves necessary to smile. Wasn't that called Moebius syndrome? Perhaps she had it.

"Nathaniel!"

The nurse whisked us to yet another cubicle, where she took Nathaniel's blood pressure, weight, and height and handed me instructions on a yellow card.

"He has a 7:30 start time. Nurse him for the last time at 3:30. That's *a.m.* Nothing after that. NOTHING. Okay? Not even water."

I nodded quickly.

"Come to the hospital by 6:15. We'll take his vital signs, change him into a johnny, and then go upstairs. You can stay with him until Anesthesia puts him to sleep. Any questions?"

A snake's nest of questions coiled inside my head but only one formed itself. Why were we doing this? I used to know. Maybe Ted still did. But the nurse could not answer so I silently shook my head.

∞

On the morning of surgery, the house stirred in the predawn gloom. I woke up restless, having had had my classic anxiety dream—at college, unable to finish my senior thesis, panicked about the future. Jeremy climbed into bed, wriggling under the soft quilt between Ted and me, and asked if the doctors were going to separate his baby's fingers.

"Not today," Ted said sleepily, putting his arms around both of us. "Nathaniel will have an operation on his head."

Jeremy knew a lot about doctors and hospitals now but he was not sure what needed fixing on Nathaniel's head. It was hard to explain to adults let alone a three-year-old.

"I can clap with one hand!" Jeremy said.

He slapped his cheek, demonstrating one answer to the Zen koan.

And then the momentum of the send-off began. Charlie, who had just moved to Boston, trudged upstairs at 6 a.m. Mom insisted on taking pictures of Jeremy, Nathaniel, and Ted because they wore matching red-and-blue striped pajamas. Then I badgered Ted to hurry up. What if a giant asteroid hit the highway, slowing traffic? He got distracted by the newspapers in the recycling bin that suddenly had to be straightened. While Jeremy kissed his baby good-bye, Charlie played what sounded like a dirge on the piano, quietly so as not to wake the downstairs tenants. In an anxious stupor, we joined the early commuters and zipped down the nearly deserted roads, arriving at Children's right on time, as Ted indignantly pointed out.

Back in Pre-op, the nurse examined Nathaniel, declared him a "go," and then issued an over-sized hospital johnny that fit like a baptismal gown. At one end of the Patient Entertainment Center, Ella Fitzgerald sang on a curvaceous neon jukebox. "You say tomato. I say tomahto. Let's call the whole thing off. . . ."

"Nathaniel!"

An escort led a small pod of parents and children onto the elevator. The kids clutched their teddy bears as tightly as I clutched Nathaniel. After an eon, the number three lit up and the cold metal doors slid back. Signs posted on the wall declared that this was SURGERY.

Completely disoriented, I closely followed the escort who punched a button and led us calmly through automatic swinging doors, past big black KEEP OUT signs, to a holding area where the bustle intensified with a rich confusion of sounds. White-coats milled about while nurses, understanding the blank terror of the place, welcomed the children with stuffed animals or playing cards. We got shunted to a toy-strewn room, reserved for babies.

A school of residents darted in, like pilot fish for the senior doctors, handing out a final round of forms: for the otolaryngologist who would put tubes in

Nathaniel's ears to relieve the fluid that had built up behind the eardrums; the anesthesiologists who would paralyze and resurrect him; the reconstructive surgeon; and the neurosurgeon who would separate the bone from the brain.

"Why can't the reconstructive surgeon do that?" Ted asked.

"Each specialty has its own territory," said the resident. "Anything that touches the brain is done by the neurosurgeon. The reconstructive surgeon knows how to do it but he would be liable if anything went wrong."

And everything and anything can go wrong, I thought. Murphy's Law.

At 8 o'clock sharp, Dr. Mulliken made his entrance, dressed in a comfortable tweed jacket and tie, not scrubs, looking more like an absent-minded English professor than a surgeon.

"Oh, Anesthesia has to put him to sleep first," he said. "That takes almost an hour. Then Otolaryngology looks at his ears. How's he doing? How are you, little fellow?"

"A little congested," Ted said as Nathaniel fussed.

"We worked late last night on the computer, planning this surgery," Dr. Mulliken said brightly, as if he had been playing Nintendo with our baby's head. He seemed exceptionally jolly for this hour of the day. He also appeared oblivious to everything except Nathaniel's skull bones. "First time."

Dr. Mulliken had given us a little peptalk, the gist of which was that the craniectomy was anything but routine. Like all experienced surgeons, he continued to search for ways to do it better, focusing his latest hopes on the computer. At Children's, the team had recently set up one of a few craniofacial computer programs in the country. Where should the bones of the skull be cut? How far forward should they be moved? With what should they be anchored? Typically, the craniofacial surgeons made those decisions in the operating room—they improvised—although that particular word offended Dr. Mulliken.

But, as Dr. Mulliken explained, the advent of computer software able to create and store a three-dimensional graphic representation of the skin and bones, the head and face, was changing how craniofacial doctors worked. Working from a CAT scan that created a picture of Nathaniel's skull, the doctors had spent last night rehearsing today's operation, viewing his bones from different angles, trying out ideas. Eventually, the team would create a topographical map of "average" faces, with three-dimensional coordinates of facial landmarks. Some day that information might be used to make a surgical template to guide the surgeon's hand in the operating room, a prediction that science journalists had been hearing for years.

Of course, an individual's face is unique, never average. But facial bones do share landmarks. Put your index fingers at your temples and you feel the temporal bone. Move your hand across your eyebrows, you feel the supra-orbital rim or eyebrow ridge. If you sweep the palm of your hand across the forehead, that is the frontal bone. The bump at the back of the skull is the occiput. The mandible, or U-shaped jawbone, carries the bottom teeth and separately hinges to the cranium by means of the zygomatic arch, right in front of the ears. The eyes hide inside bony sockets or orbits. The gap between the eyes, over the bridge of the nose, is the intra-orbital distance. The midface goes from the bottom of the eyes to the top row of teeth and includes the cheekbones. The brain sits inside the braincase, which occupies the top half of the skull.

(Ever since scientists discovered the first human fossils in the 1850s, they have scrutinized skulls, hoping to pinpoint what makes us human. Apes have larger braincases, foreheads that slope back, protruding muzzles, powerful jaws, parabolically curved palates, a foramen magnum—or opening for the spinal cord toward the rear of the skull—better for quadripeds. Humans have smaller braincases, high rounded foreheads, lightly built lower jaws, U-shaped palates, delicate teeth, shorter, flatter faces, and a foramen magnum right under the skull base—better for bipeds.)

The bones of the skull and face are not sculpted from one large block but constructed from components. The skull is made of several main plates, which grow together at junctions called sutures. The sutures, which look like squiggly lines, are the places where the bony plates literally knit together. Typically, the skull's sutures are "open" when the baby is first born but fuse during the first two years of life.

The face also has its own components. Emergency room doctors know from treating drunks who black out and fall face first on hard pavement that the face tends to break along the lines where its components got stitched and pleated together. But interestingly, these components grow at different rates. In the first years of life, the skull grows very fast to accommodate the rapidly developing brain. The forehead reaches its peak growth by the age of eight. The mid-face stops growing by twelve or fourteen. The jaw stops growing last. Craniofacial doctors try to time surgical intervention to this natural growth cycle.

The computer qualified as a wonderful and powerful tool for dealing with the complexities of the skull and face. But because craniofacial surgery was still in pioneering phases, Dr. Mulliken's lineage inspired more confidence than any gadgetry. He had learned his trade from the previous director of the Craniofacial Centre, a Nobel Prize winner named Joseph Murray, who had learned from *le grand maître,* Paul Tessier himself.

Tessier was a legend, an icon, and the founder of craniofacial surgery. Until 1957 the craniofacial region was, surgically speaking, no man's land. That changed when Tessier met a young man whom he later described as having "one of the worst manifestations of Crouzon syndrome" he had ever seen. (Like Apert syndrome, Crouzon affects the bones of the face and skull. However, it does not affect the hands or feet.) Galled by his inability to help, the young doctor boarded a train from Paris to Nantes, where he had gone to medical school. There he dissected cadavers, working with an assistant until two in the morning, finding ways to advance the bones in the face and use grafts to stabilize them in their new position. Later, he would say that his passion for big game hunting sharpened the excellent sense of orientation that facial surgery required. Tessier slowly shifted from cadavers to people. And in 1970, Tessier published his first reports and invited doctors from around the world to Paris to see what he had invented.

Dr. Mulliken coughed, jarring us back to the present. He explained that he would move the supra-orbital rim forward and anchor it somewhere near the temples, depending on the state and condition of the bone.

"What do you use?" Ted asked.

"Titanium screws," Dr. Mulliken answered.

"Is he going to set off airport security?"

"Nah. If I can, I'll try to pull the bridge of his nose forward but sometimes the bone is awfully small there. Kids with Apert are often big here," he indicated just above the temples, making blinkers with his hands. "I might try to shave that down."

Had we given consent to a nose job? He talked as if Nathaniel was made of plasticene. To Mulliken, anatomy was not destiny, just a rough draft. Everything seemed adjustable. Move the eyes closer together or farther apart? Nose up or out? Mustard or mayo?

Nathaniel had just turned three months old. He had reached that wondrous stage where we could look in his eyes and connect. The bond of mutual gazing was intoxicating. This would surely set him back. Nathaniel worked contentedly on his pacifier, unable to anticipate what might come next.

The OR nurse tapped her watch. "It's time."

"By the way," coughed Dr. Mulliken. "I have a request from public affairs. A photographer wants to take pictures today in the OR for a book on surgeons."

"Sure," I looked at Ted, who shrugged. "As long as Nathaniel is not recognizable."

"A last one for me," said Dr. Mulliken, opening his shoulder-hanging camera case.

I held Nathaniel in my arms, feeling his downy skin, as Dr. Mulliken snapped what would surely be "Before" in his medical notebook.

"Will he go with me?" asked the OR nurse.

"One last picture," I repeated, wanting to remember for different reasons.

Ted cradled Nathaniel, his big arms wrapped snugly before he gave Nathaniel one last squeeze and turned him over to the waiting nurse.

"Take good care of him," I demanded.

"I love you," said Ted, the color gone from his face.

Nathaniel stretched his soft, round arms towards me.

"Say, bye-bye, see you soon," the OR nurse chuckled. "You'll do fine. Just fine. Won't you little guy?"

I sank into the rocking chair while Ted knelt next to me, burying his head in my shoulder. Through my tears, I saw a sterile, disposable place with hard sharp corners.

"Let's go home," said Ted. "I would rather wait there."

"I don't want to leave the hospital," I protested.

"They can call us if they need us. We're only fifteen minutes away."

The nurse overheard us arguing and interrupted, "Don't go. This is a big deal."

"Tell my husband, please."

"I don't want to scare him."

"We are scared anyway."

∞

We slunk off to the official Family Waiting Area, adjacent to the operating rooms, which even at this hour of the day, reeked with anxiety.

"I'm Brenda, the liaison nurse this morning." She had that professionally perky voice that flight attendants used to have. "And what surgery is Dr. Mulliken doing today?"

"A craniectomy," Ted said.

"I call the OR every hour and half for an update. Dr. Mulliken usually finishes around supper time, sometimes later," she said as she checked Nathaniel's name off her clipboard. "Take a beeper if you want to leave the waiting area."

Downstairs across the crowded lobby, I caught sight of a child with Apert syndrome and recognized Ruth but ducked my head. A lifetime had passed since our summer meeting, and now, on the day of Nathaniel's first operation, I was afraid to get too close, as if her bad luck might rub off on us. At the twenty-four-hour falafel stand outside the hospital's entrance, Ted complained about a headache while I worried that my milk was drying up.

"Isn't that Dr. Smith?" I asked. Dr. Smith was the otolaryngologist who was going to examine Nathaniel's ears. "He's supposed to be in the OR with Nathaniel."

Dr. Smith stood next to a couple of ambulance drivers, chomping down on something hot.

"He must have finished," I said.

He took another bite.

"How did everything go, Dr. Smith?" I asked.

He looked blank.

"Nathaniel Finch?" Ted said.

"What's he in for?"

"A craniectomy." That word again.

"Oh no," he said, wiping his fingers before he ran off, surgical clogs clacking on the pavement.

In the waiting area, the hopelessness swelled without something concrete and useful to do, so Ted thumbed quarterly reports, inspecting cash flow and earnings, and then complained to his doctor about a persistent headache. Every three hours, in prayer-like ritual, I retreated to a cubicle with a rocking chair and breast pump and dutifully filled a plastic container with blueish milk which got dated, labeled, and stored in a freezer. In between, I sewed.

The women in our extended family had organized a quilt project in Nathaniel's honor. My square was July, a homey scene with a chair and cupboard, made by sewing infuriatingly tiny x's of colored thread on a cloth grid. Like most of the others who had the other eleven months, I was daunted by the scope and intricacy of the undertaking. Aunt EJ, Mom's partner in the project, was the exception, the only one who actually knew what she was doing.

Besides keeping us busy, the quilt was an expression of sisterhood and a reflection of Nathaniel's impact on family cosmology. He had broken the sound barrier that once existed about my aunt's "handicap," whose most remarkable feature, in retrospect, was its transparency. I neither thought about her difference nor considered it very important.

My mother had grown up with the same attitude. As a child, Mom ran off to play tennis or go horseback riding, never thinking why her big sister stayed behind with the grown-ups. Beyond the carelessness of youth was silence, aided by my grandmother's distaste for standing out in a crowd and the fact that a skirt hid my aunt's unusual leg for most of her life.

As a child, I knew that my aunt was missing a leg. She had wonderful common sense and made so little fuss that I assumed everyone had an aunt like mine. But the inattention disguised what made her unique. I had my first inkling of how little I really understood about my aunt when I was ten. In the summer when we visited, Ganny made the hour-long drive from Berkeley, past the mysterious San Quentin prison to Aunt EJ and Uncle Les's house in Belvedere. While Ganny ironed, I swam with my cousins in the lagoon on which the house was built. Accustomed to sweet lakewater, I found the yellow-green lagoon with its barnacles and the slimy stuff clinging to the wooden ladder and the deck frightening. When my feet inadvertently touched bottom, they made contact with something crunchy and then sank into endless muck. Swimming was the only salvation but invariably I forgot to keep my mouth closed and swallowed the brine, gagging at its salty taste.

One day after a swim, I was lying on a towel on the deck, drying off, when I heard the slow, rhythmic and familiar click of EJ's crutches on the house's cool slab floor. Early in the morning and late in the evening, EJ wore a floor-length bathrobe, belt-tied in the middle. Her wooden leg—plastic really—was off, leaning against something in the corner of her bedroom. With a shoe and stocking, like a mannequin's.

When the crutches thudded on the deck, I looked up and stared at Aunt EJ, who was wearing a bathing suit. Her strong complete leg bulged with strength and her body listed to that side. Her stump ended just above where the knee would have been, swinging gently like a boat at anchor. She reached the swimming ladder, and, oblivious to the slime, lowered herself into the lagoon, where she stroked across the waves. The very act of swimming with one leg baffled and mystified me. I looked away, embarrassed by my need to stare yet fascinated. I was frightened by the loss that her leg suggested, afraid to discover the truth, that loss is part of everyone's life. Questions clouded my head. Was it okay to stare? How did she swim? What was it like? Aunt EJ got out of the water but I had no idea how to respectfully ask my questions until twenty years later when Nathaniel was born.

"I had to look and appear as normal as possible," Aunt EJ wrote. "Clothes were always the right length to cover the leg mechanisms. I wore long stockings. Always. I was sent to special dancing classes and went along because I didn't want to look different. But several years ago, I saw a young girl amputee crossing the street in shorts and bare legs! It flashed through my mind that I would like to have been so unconcerned. It took a long time to become unselfconscious."

Aunt EJ drew her greatest support from her father, who encouraged her independence literally by design. Before she got her prosthetic leg, her father built a trike she could pedal herself, folding crutches, and, in the 1940s, a manually operated brake and clutch system for the steering column of the family car. After she'd graduated from the University of California, he supported her efforts to get a degree in occupational therapy in Boston. She was encouraged to be good with her hands because with the cumbersome prosthetic technology of the times, it was hard to be mobile or agile with her feet. Most of all, he urged her to "believe that she could conquer anything, to know that she was loved."

∾

The OR liaison nurse had to be the most excruciatingly polite person employed outside the diplomatic corps. Nathaniel was "asleep" by 9:30. By 11:00, the first incision had been made. By 12:30, the neurosurgeon was hard at work. From 2:00 on, Dr. Mulliken "harvested bone." By 5:00, he moved the forehead. At 6:30, he was ready to "close up," which made Nathaniel sound like a deli. Dr. Mulliken emerged, as predicted, at 7:30.

"Everything went as well as could be expected," he said. "I moved the supraorbital rim forward. Couldn't get that small piece at the bridge of his nose but I'll get that later when I do the mid-face."

Nathaniel was alive. The words functioned as spatial co-ordinates, fixing a location on the shapeless and fundamentally incomprehensible activities of the day.

"We patched the dura," he said as if ticking down a grocery list. "That's the tough outer covering of the brain. His was pretty thin in spots. He still has some openings in his skull but the bone will grow over in time." Dr. Mulliken sat down. Was he always this exhausted? Or disappointed?

"Nathaniel had a long bleeding time. That should get checked out further. He also has three fused sutures, which is unusual. He'll probably need a back of the head operation later," he said.

Another operation? I froze in silent panic, suddenly aching for a third child who faced nothing more complicated than a runny nose. Ted bombarded Dr. Mulliken with questions, seeking clarification and the companionship of dialog until Dr. Mulliken called a friendly halt, saying, "Let's see how he gets through this one first."

I bolted to my feet. Now, more than anything else, I wanted to cut loose and see our baby. As I shook Dr. Mulliken's hand, I tried to forget where it had been all day.

We are Quaker, like William Penn who we studied this year. The kids and grown-ups sit quietly. It is our Tradition to talk to God that way.

# Chapter Seven

✥

# Crossing the Line

In the intensive care unit, Ted and I took stock of the enormity of the changes that had taken place, despairing at the sight of our baby's tiny body, inert and espaliered on the bed. The body is in perpetual motion until the moment of death, to which this came perilously close. Under the bright fluorescent light, Nathaniel's skin looked chartreuse. A turban of snowy white bandages wrapped around his forehead mercifully concealed the long incision. Cool pads covered his eyes while cotton plugged his ears. Out of his mouth came a breathing tube, secured in place with a piece of surgical tape across his cheek. An IV was inserted near his wrist, and on his big toe, the red light of the oximeter shone. Nathaniel's EKG, respiratory rate, and heart rate blipped by on the computer screen. A clear tube snaked out of the leg of his diaper, emptying urine into a plastic bag at the base of the crib.

"Can we lift that?" Ted asked, meaning the bandages on his head.

"Oh no no no," protested the night nurse. "No one touches Dr. Mulliken's work."

Ted wrapped his arm about my shoulder while I slid mine around his waist. He had spent time in intensive care when he fractured his neck, and, while this place stirred a fleeting recollection, I knew he took comfort that Nathaniel would have no memory of his sojourn. My body grieved from a day without a baby in the crook of my arm or suckling my breasts and now it was impossible to even stroke his skin because so much was stuck in it. Finally, Ted and I took turns placing our hands on a postage stamp-sized area on his thigh.

"I thought that I'd stop by and check on Nathaniel," said a familiar voice. I spun around, pleased at this late hour to see the geneticist, who did not usually work at Children's.

"How did he do?" she asked.

Ted shrugged.

"You look beat," she said. "Go home."

Ted searched my face but I shook my head vehemently, not yet ready to leave.

"No. I have to make sure that it's Nathaniel, you know, be positive that they've got the right guy." I tried to joke but the geneticist wasn't buying it.

"You have read too many novels," she huffed. With brisk detachment, the geneticist conferred with the doctor on duty and then before discreetly bowing out, she urged gently, "Go home. Get some sleep."

We whispered I-love-yous in Nathaniel's cotton-plugged ears and then fled down the corridors, into the parking lot, down the dark streets where sodium-vapor streetlights looked like lemon drops. Mom met us at the top of the stairs, restless as a ghost. The words exchanged seemed puny and insufficient. We fell into bed.

When the alarm rang at 2 a.m., I pumped my breasts and dialed the ICU.

"Pavilion Five," the receptionist said flatly. I whispered Nathaniel's name before she transferred me to the nurse, who chatted like an amused baby sitter to an overprotective parent. I hung up, transferred the breast milk to the freezer, and lurched back upstairs only to discover that Jeremy had crept into our bed, already asleep. Tonight I would not carry him back to his own. We needed each other too much.

∾

The stack of newspapers on the breakfast table confirmed that time marched on elsewhere even if it stopped for us. The sight of Mom eating a baked root vegetable from a South American country—she was a health food nut from way back, a muesli and yogurt eater in my childhood—further anchored my tenuous sense of reality. So did Jeremy, who materialized, wearing red boots and one pair of pajama bottoms on his bottom and another on his head, his pretend version of long hair.

"Bang!" he said, making his piece of toast into a gun. "Got you, Grandma Julia."

She withered, not needing much to pretend.

"How about a hug?" I said to Jeremy. He obligingly leaned his cheek closer.

"How are you?" asked Mom. She looked as if she had not slept.

"In a stupor," I said.

"Where's Nathaniel?" Jeremy asked, his velvet brown eyes alert with a child's unswerving intuition that something was wrong.

That seemed like a cosmic question, on a par with what killed the dinosaurs, how did life spontaneously generate, and what is its meaning and purpose. But since Jeremy was sensitive to perturbations in our family's emotional atmosphere, I tried for his sake to keep an even keel and pretend that the complex was actually simple.

"Sleeping at the hospital," I said.

"Why?" Jeremy pressed.

I tackled that one with a firm "Because" and then added, "You will see him after school. Grandma Julia will bring you."

"Fine. How's Ted?" Mom said, struggling to keep her anxiety under control.

"He's in the shower, washing off yesterday," I said, hoping to do the same myself.

"I'm going to see Daddy," Jeremy declared. He disappeared, trailing a PeeWee Herman doll, a freebie from the year Ted invested in toy companies.

Mom spoke quietly, "I called him Charlie all day yesterday. He's been so full of energy that I rigged a punching bag on the bunk bed. By the way, he bit a child at nursery school. The teacher sounded very nice; she'll fill you in at your conference."

I shook my head, overwhelmed.

"I was a biter and a screamer. Ask Aunt Ruthie about the potato I threw at her. I had terrible tantrums, kicking, screaming on the floor," Mom reassured me. "He's fine. All things considered."

∞

"Which do you want?" asked the nurse whom I stopped in the hallway, having forgotten the way to intensive care. "Cardiac, neonate, or med-surge?"

"The last," I guessed, having naively assumed that there was only one. Up a cavernous flight of stairs and down an endless corridor, Ted and I stumbled on cardiac intensive care. After a few wrong turns, Ted found a janitor who guided us to double doors where a hand-written sign instructed all visitors to stop at the front desk.

"Can't you read?" the receptionist barked as I trespassed over the piece of bright orange adhesive tape that marked a line on the floor.

"I'm looking for my baby!" I yelled, fighting back tears.

"Nathaniel Finch?" Ted said, urgently leaning over the counter to read the papers on her desk. She glared and then checked her color-coded chart, tersely apologizing that Nathaniel was not here.

"Well, where is he?" Ted hissed.

She vanished and a short time later, reappeared, looking menacingly at us. "Are you his parents?"

"Yes."

She operated an intercom, slamming down the button on a bulbous microphone to activate the loudspeaker at the bedspace, where, according to her supervisor, Nathaniel was supposed to be.

"Can Mom and Dad go back?" she asked in a clipped voice and then closed her eyes, waiting for the answer to crackle back.

"Another five minutes," said the intercom.

The clock read 8:00 a.m., too early to deal with this sadist. Beyond the desk, the Unit hummed—an efficient colony of white-coats that suggested intensive care was the emergency room, only in slow motion.

"Take a seat in there," the receptionist ordered. "I'll call YOU."

Banished to the waiting area, where droopy-eyed adults sprawled across couches under a yammering TV, we flopped momentarily, but then, twitching with anxiety, electric with impatience, returned to the bright orange line on the floor.

"What's taking so long?" Ted demanded.

She gave that Medical-Standard-Time shrug and shuffled paperwork across her desk before giving the approving nod. We plodded to Nathaniel's crib.

"He looks worse," Ted said flatly.

"Really?" The name-tag on the day nurse's scrub-suit read Annemarie.

Nathaniel was puffed up like an over-inflated tire with purple blotches decorating his greenish skin and so much fluid in his eyelids that one had flipped inside out. Ted put the eyelid pad back but it did not stay.

"Has Dr. Mulliken come by?" Ted pushed. "He has seen this? What did he say?"

"I don't know Dr. Mulliken," said Annemarie, who wore a small gold cross around her neck. She looked too young to drive a car, much less operate all this sophisticated machinery. I prayed that God would be helping out. "What operation did he do again?"

"A craniectomy," I said, hating the word.

"What's this?" Ted demanded.

"That's the ventilator. The vent is breathing for him because his airway is swollen from surgery," she said.

"When does that breathing tube come out?" I asked, knowing nothing about ventilators except that I loathed them.

"I'm not sure. Just a second," Annemarie called to the nurse in the adjacent bed and reported back. "Peak swelling is forty-eight hours after surgery, tapering off after seventy-two hours. They might extubate him to-morrow or the day after."

Nathaniel made a sound that struck my ears the way a high-pitched whistle hits a dog.

"Is he in pain? Are you giving him anything?"

"He's had morphine, Fentanyl, and also Versed—it's a new drug, a short-acting sedative to keep him calm."

"A sedative?" I asked, incredulous. Ibuprofen was the strongest drug in our medicine cabinet.

"The natural tendency is to fight the vent. The older kids say it is the worst part of the Unit," she said.

"Then let's get it out," Ted declared, as if it was suddenly very simple what had to be done.

She looked askance. "It's not our call."

"Then whose is it?" Ted asked.

"I'm not sure," said Annemarie, who finally comprehended the tortured confusion in our eyes. "Sorry. This is my first day on the job. I'm still learning the ropes."

∾

Ted paged Dr. Mulliken, who, fifteen minutes later, sauntered into intensive care, whistling.

"How's our little friend?" he clucked, leaning over the crib.

"Our little friend is turning colors and his lids are flipping inside out," Ted pointed out. "When is that vent coming out?"

Dr. Mulliken was genuinely surprised at Ted's agitation and then placating. "It's all perfectly normal, second day, post-op phenomenon. Keep the lids covered. And the vent. . . . That will be out maybe today, probably tomorrow, no problem."

When Dr. Mulliken carefully snipped the bandages off, he was engrossed, inspecting his handiwork, especially the incision circumnavigating Nathaniel's skull which started in front of one ear and followed the polar route over the top of his head to the front of his other ear. It was held together with black threads—like a line of marching ants. (Certain Amazonian Indian tribes actually decapitated black ants and used their sharp mandibles for the ultimate in ecologically friendly, self-dissolving sutures.)

The faces of all children change but none as suddenly or radically as Nathaniel's. Ted and I stared, speechless, absorbing the new configuration, just as we had at birth, just as we had stared at the medical photos in Dr. Mulliken's office. Nathaniel was shaved bald; his black infant hair, complete with dandruff and skin flakes had been saved in a baggy by a thoughtful nurse. The presence of an eyebrow ridge that smoothed away the old hatband mark transformed the topography of Nathaniel's face. Instead of towering, his forehead sloped back at a gentle new angle. His eyes no longer popped out but dwelled within the safe caverns of bony orbits. His nose was small, stubbier and swollen.

Examined dispassionately, the shifts were small—a centimeter or two or three—but taken together in the gestalt of the face, the emotional impact was immeasurable. Nathaniel's post-op face was nowhere near as beautiful as his pre-op face but that was because he was too sedated to animate this version. The craniofacial team's administrator confided that one mother had screamed at Dr. Mulliken after the first surgery, ordering him to undo the operation. I did not hate Nathaniel's new face. It was just too new to trust that it really belonged to him.

"I wish I had been able to get his nose. Just couldn't. Well . . . next time," Dr. Mulliken muttered and then glanced up, peering at Ted. "You have a very small bridge. And it looks like you broke your nose. Sports?"

"Hockey stick," Ted said.

"I can fix that if you want," Dr. Mulliken said nicely. Then he wrapped a new set of bandages, instructing Annemarie about the proper placement and tension with the fastidious of a virtuoso. "Don't hesitate to call. I'm here until 8 tonight."

Ted left for work and I had my mission, having decided that if our baby was fighting the vent, then so were we. I planned to infiltrate behind the lines, but unlike the NICU at Beth Israel, this intensive care was intentionally obscure, impersonal, and hard to penetrate. The place had no formal sign and its name shifted from speaker to speaker. The receptionist answered the phone: "Pavilion Five," the nurses on duty called it "The Unit" and sometimes "the ICU," and our friends referred to "Intensive Care." Whatever the name, the receptionist controlled access as if it were a maximum security facility. Each time I appeared at the orange tape line on the floor—even after regular trips to pump my breasts—she frisked me with her eyes, searching for signs of emotional crack-up. I might have given in to the impulse except that Annemarie was my worst fear: a novice taking care of my son. She needed baby sitting, which meant that squeamishness was suddenly an unaffordable luxury.

Every hour or so, overtaken by a sense of futility, I sang into Nathaniel's ear, so that he could hear the sound of my voice, certain that even in his unconscious state, he sensed my presence. But I also sang for the same reason that people whistle in the dark, to keep the burgeoning fear at bay. Between "I've Been Working on the Railroad" and "You are My Sunshine," two friends appeared next to the crib. The receptionist enforced the rules that allowed only the immediate family and then one visitor at a time, but I had instructed Lynnie and Gish to say that they were out-of-town cousins.

"Isn't that sweet?" Lynnie said, meaning my little concert.

"I thought it was sad," Gish blurted out.

"I hate pity," I said abruptly.

"Why?" she asked. "The nuns taught that it was like tenderness or compassion."

"For me, it's a way to keep distance. "

More than anything, I wanted people to identify, connect, and bond with our baby just as we had. Pity was sorrow but without the empathetic connection, sadness minus the involvement with the person who suffers. I watched the expressions on my friends' faces. When Nathaniel was first born, I was struck by how unpredictably people reacted and now it was just the opposite. They both winced and then looked queasy. What was the matter with keeping some distance? Maybe I would be better off if I could too.

∽

When Mom brought Jeremy to intensive care, he was so excited by a caterpillar tractor snowplow that he had seen in the parking lot that it wasn't until he was in my arms, hovering over the crib, that his face puckered in fear.

"I want to go home," he declared, echoing my own thoughts.

Jeremy thought that Nathaniel might like to hear music from "Beauty and the Beast" so he pushed the button and left the tape player running next to the urine bag.

When Charlie dropped by, I offered him a bite of Snickers.

"Not with my high cholesterol," he demurred.

"That's too bad," I said, placing the pad back on Nathaniel's swollen eyelid.

"I walk inside a hospital, think I'm going to have a heart attack, and you act like this is no big deal," he gestured at the surroundings to which clarity of purpose had temporarily blinded me.

"All kids are, by definition, reasons for parents to worry. He just pushes the envelope in a major way," I joked, trying to make light of the tension.

"You are born to bluff," Charlie observed sadly. "Don't you ever fall apart?"

I thought of all the things that needed to be done, grateful for the physical demands that babies make.

"I don't know what else to do," I replied.

Mom insisted on taking pictures.

"I can't stand family albums that only include happy events. Such a false memory. Do you know that no one takes photographs at funerals?"

"Mom," I gritted my teeth. "This isn't a funeral."

"I know," she said, irritated by nit-picking. At least Mom had something to do. I blushed as she snapped away, treating Nathaniel's crib like a historical monument or a panoramic sunset in the background. Then we retreated downstairs and sat in the hospital's outside cafeteria, enjoying the Indian summer day, the inviting golden tint to the October light, until Jeremy kicked a birch tree.

"Don't rip the bark," I yelled. "Please!"

Jeremy wore purple sweat pants and a devilish, I-dare-you-to-stop-me expression on his round face. He was verbal, intense, and too clever for his own good sometimes. We were not going to be able to keep up with this child.

"Is Jeremy going to be a juvenile delinquent?" I asked Mom. Every time I floated this worry, Ted assured me that he had been a strong-willed child.

"No," she said.

"Do you think he's acting up because Nathaniel's in intensive care?" That morning, Jeremy had thrown King Neptune's toy trident at Ted, who took it away. Half an hour later, when Jeremy wanted it again, he bit me in a rage, then asked defiantly, "Are you going to take my teeth away?"

"Just having a baby brother is hard," she soothed.

Jeremy had not suggested sending Nathaniel back to the hospital the way that some siblings do when a baby is born. Maybe he wished it secretly and every time Nathaniel went to the hospital, Jeremy figured that his dark desire had come true.

"You were all right, weren't you?" I asked Mom.

"Yes," Mom said, wanting to ease my worries and then catching herself on the truth. "No. I called my sister Queen Eleanora behind her back because she never got in any trouble. And I always did. My parents expected me to be perfect. But you won't do that."

But that was exactly what I was doing. When one child's needs consumed so much parental energy, the other got lost in the shuffle.

"Paula got to you, is that it?" Mom asked.

I shrugged, seeing Jeremy hide under the bushes, right in front of the sign that read, "Stay on the path." He looked me straight in the eye, testing. I looked at Mom instead, saying, "Nice sweater."

"It doesn't really fit me," she replied. "Would you like it?"

I ignored Jeremy's defiance and wet a napkin to wash off the food stain on my own shirt. "It won't always be like this, will it?"

Mom embraced my disheveled state with a reassuring gaze. "Oh no no. Kids grow up fast. Even Nathaniel."

"I meant you picking out my clothes," I teased.

∾

When Ted returned to the hospital in the evening, he was alarmed to see how little Nathaniel had improved and paged Dr. Mulliken, who arrived minus saunter and whistle nearly an hour later.

"What's the plan for getting him off the vent?" Ted asked.

Dr. Mulliken cut him off with a curt reprimand, "He's still swollen. You can see that for yourselves."

"But you said today, maybe tomorrow."

"I can't give you a precise minute," he sighed. "It's only been what? 24 hours? Besides it's not my call."

That was news. "Whose is it?"

"The ICU doctor," he said in a cool tone. Who the hell was the ICU doctor? Between the nurses, respiratory therapists, attending physicians, fellows, X-ray technicians, chaplains, medical students, and janitors, there were more actors here than in a Broadway musical. We needed a picture and biography to keep everyone straight.

"We're doing everything we can," Dr. Mulliken said. "Let's see how he does tomorrow. Go home, get some rest. I need to."

Dr. Mulliken spun on his heels. He practically lived at the hospital, putting in fourteen-hour days, seven days a week and ranked as one of the top craniofacial surgeons in the country. He had a surfeit of optimism and damn-the-torpedoes attitude needed in this line of work but this was the second time that he fudged the bad news.

"The vent is no big deal for Dr. Mulliken," Ted observed. "Not when you make faces for a living."

The din of the Unit washed over my ears: information-giving adult voices against a discordant counterpoint of dings, beeps, shrieks—all the racket signaling that Nathaniel was out of kilter. Just as Ted pushed the tape button on a maudlin section of "Beauty and the Beast," his brother Mat materialized next to the crib, wearing his doctor pajamas from work. So that was how he managed to slip past the receptionist!

"How's Bambino?" He read the failure in our faces and then thumbed the flow charts, deciphering the medications and dosages, with the reassurance that despite the ripe aroma of anesthesia, despite his drug-fogged state, Nathaniel still belonged to us.

∽

Halloween, especially at Children's Hospital, was a welcome holiday from the usual tyranny of appearance, when no one mistook a person's true identity for the mask he wore. Jeremy, who was too young to equate the day with candy, vacillated between being the Little Mermaid or a warrior, settling finally on a black-hatted witch with a twig-broom. Ted opted for sheet-ghost, while I stayed in character with Nathaniel, charmed by the children who ignored casts, bandages, and IV poles and dressed up to trick or treat the nurses' stations.

"Good news," said the head anesthesiologist, who was wearing a bright yellow clown wig and red clown nose. "We're going to try and extubate him today."

"Can I be there?" I asked, surprised. This was the first time I had seen the head anesthesiologist in intensive care. Wasn't this decision supposed to be made by the chief ICU doctor? It was impossible to keep the chain of command straight, much less the multitude of individuals involved. The more the merrier, I thought. Besides, extubation equaled exhilaration.

"Oh no," he said firmly and apologetically. "It's the rule. Parents have to leave when we do a procedure."

The intensive care staff got busy with emergencies so that it was noon when I got exiled to the waiting room to sit with our new baby sitter, who was helping out ten hours a week while getting a master's in public health. Before going back to school, she had been a respiratory therapist in a neonatal intensive care unit, which at the moment qualified her as an angel. Instead of sharing our belligerent attitude toward the vent, she called the play-by-play without actually seeing the action. But as the minutes tugged along, I stamped over to the receptionist to find out what was happening.

"They're working," she said, stone-faced.

After forty-five minutes, the head anesthesiologist shuffled into the family waiting room, wig askew.

"We did everything—propped him, gave him oxygen—but he just wasn't making it. We'll try again in a couple of days."

My hopes collapsed. In Mexico, Halloween is celebrated as the Day of the Dead, a special time when the thin veil that separates the world of the living from the dead lifts, allowing all spirits to mingle and communicate. I had hoped that this Halloween the portal between Nathaniel's world and ours would open. Ted had been so ecstatic about extubation that the word rolled joyfully off his tongue and now I dreaded telling him that Nathaniel was not ready to return.

∾

Two days later, the breathing tube came out and Nathaniel woke up and cried miserably. He behaved as if he had the world's worst headache, which he probably did. He left the Unit's limbo for Eight West, one of several recuperation wings for children under the age of three. Nathaniel was assigned to a four-pack, a room with four beds and no privacy, on a floor with a sunny playroom and a kitchen stocked—as Jeremy quickly discovered—with a limitless supply of popsicles and jello. While we barely noticed the other kids in intensive care, our roommates now prompted stares and questions. One little girl had scalded her leg in the bathtub when the landlord accidentally turned the water heater on too high. She refused to let go of her mother, especially at night. Like a bloodhound, she sniffed a medical person hundreds of feet away and although the nurses took off their white coats before entering the room, she screamed so much that her voice dissolved into a hoarse bark.

An invisible child was surrounded by Cambodian parents, aunties, uncles, brothers, sisters, and cousins who spoke no English. At night, the whole family wanted to sleep in the hospital but the nurse held up one finger and mouthed the words slowly: Only one person allowed. In the end, one became two as the mother and a cousin slept in the chair that unfolded into a narrow cot.

A one-year-old boy slept in a mist tent, a clear plastic contraption that completely covered his crib, barking with pneumonia and whimpering whenever his teen-aged mother left him. She appeared in the evenings, bored and listless, watched TV, and told him to pipe down.

"Why doesn't she stay with her kid?" I whispered to Ted.

"Maybe she can't."

"Where's the dad?"

"Probably not around."

"There's a kid on the floor who actually lives here," I said. "A boy named Adam. It's bad enough for a week. All your life? I don't see his parents either. I'd never leave Nathaniel," I said as Ted arranged the tubes just so. "Never."

Ted nodded slowly. If he could have nursed Nathaniel, he would have. From the day of Nathaniel's birth, he understood what the bond meant to me, and envied it.

∞

A week later, the first big O was over. Ted and I found ourselves in a pizza joint with the children, savoring the newfound pleasure in the simple act of eating out. Jeremy sat in a grown-up chair, his chin level with the table-top. For such a small person, he had an astonishingly large appetite. Nathaniel rested peacefully in Ted's arms. His face was returning to something that approximated normal and although it was not his original, it was close enough. Oddly enough, his once jet-black hair was now growing in blonde. Had Dr. Mulliken inadvertently fiddled with that too?

"When will Nathaniel eat pizza?" Jeremy asked.

"When he gets teeth," I said.

Jeremy bared his own. This family outing felt like parole from prison. Although friends were reluctant to compare their woes of blocked chimneys or irate bosses to the barbaric incarceration that Nathaniel had just endured, I desperately needed to talk about ordinary things.

"So what do *you* think about Charlie and Trish?" I asked Ted.

"I hope they get married," Ted said. "Trish is a gem."

"She is," I said. Nathaniel acted as an informal Rorschach test for character. People responded to him a wide variety of ways: some approached cautiously, while others drew back in fear; some asked a ton of questions, while others barely batted an eye. Trish responded with simple and instinctual warmth, but in the hospital, she had also proved to be a woman after my own heart, sympathetic to those twin pillars of crisis management: chocolate and junk magazines.

"Do you think that they are too different?" I asked.

"No. They seem compatible to me," Ted replied.

Charlie, I suspected, was cautious because marriage, like blood transfusion, was a matter of finding the right match. What two living things need to make a healthy union pivots on the intriguing question of just how different is different.

"Who's getting married?" Jeremy asked.

"No one yet," I said, and then impatient to eat, fingered a swelling on Nathaniel's head. "Is this bigger?

The leathery folds of skin on Nathaniel's head had knit together and everyone had the same impulse: to stroke his stubble, soothe away the imagined pain, discern the significance of the holes and bumps, and like phrenologists, divine the future. But one bump stuck out more than the others.

"Yes. It does seem bigger," Ted said, touching his fingers on one of the holes in Nathaniel's skull.

"You can feel his brain pulsing," I told Ted.

"Don't keep pushing on it," he replied, before trying himself. "I don't know. If you look at anything long enough, it looks strange."

"Isn't that our neonatalogist?" I suddenly said, waving across the noisy babble of the restaurant, happy to see her. When she came over to our table, I thought grimly that it was a bad omen when our social life revolved around Nathaniel's doctors.

"He looks terrific! And so big," she said bending down to look him in the eye. Nathaniel *was* big, compared to her usual preemie clientele, and he threw her a toothless grin for the compliment. "How's he doing?"

"Great . . . except," I glanced at Ted, who was already nodding in anticipation of my question. Another doctor who had praised Dr. Mulliken's handiwork thought the bulge was no big deal, just brain fluid, which, like the ocean, had its own high and low tides. "What do you think about this bump?"

She massaged Nathaniel's head as if washing hair in a beauty salon and then shook her head soberly, dodging the waitress who brought a steaming pizza over to the table. While Jeremy screeched with ravenous joy, she urged, "Definitely get this checked out."

∞

"Looks like fluid," mumbled Dr. Mulliken when I took Nathaniel to Children's the next day. "I would like to know what's going on. Could aspirate with a needle but . . . better have the neurosurgeon check first."

The neurosurgeon's office had spindly-legged furniture and a gallery of photos of men in white coats, boring images compared to the amazing organ from which brain specialists made a living. He sent us to the darkened room of the ultrasonagrapher knowledgeable about children with craniofacial anomalies.

"It's his brain," she said after passing her magic wand over the bulge. She made her pronouncement unambiguously, once on the phone to the neurosurgeon and twice on the phone to Dr. Mulliken. What a weird place for a brain to be, I thought. Aren't brains supposed to hide inside skulls? Then, horrified, that a needle might have been stuck there to diagnose the problem, I cradled Nathaniel with an urgent sense of protection and ran to Dr. Mulliken's office, tracking him in the hallway between suture removals.

"Good thing you didn't touch it," I said. "Why is his brain there?"

"Probably the dura—the tough outer covering of the brain—is thin. His is awfully thin," Dr. Mulliken said slowly, his trademark optimism shadowed by this setback. "This doesn't happen very often with kids with Apert. I should probably get a picture."

He opened his camera case and snapped. In the book of Before and After, this belonged to the chapter of terrible things that had almost happened. But if I allowed myself to fall into that abyss, I would never crawl back out. The good news was that terrible things had *not* happened. The complications, the fight against the respirator, the imprisonment of the ICU, the trauma of the hospital, overshadowed the fact that the first operation would allow Nathaniel's brain to grow at a critical period. Because I had the very first inkling of the standards that Dr. Mulliken applied when he said that craniofacial surgery was difficult, because I liked him better when he thought out loud and did not varnish the truth, the bump hitched us as a team, building the wary trust that we were in this together.

My Brother Jeremy came
with me to the hospital
to hold my hand when
I got my tooth Pulled.
My gum felt Like a
hard brick wall. It did
not hurt but it was
bloody. My Brother looked
in my mouth and thought
it was disgusting.

# Chapter Eight

❧

# The ℋolidays

*November and December 1990*

As darkness engulfed New England's northern latitudes, things slowly fell apart. In a contrarian mood, Ted and I hosted a Thanksgiving that did not feature turkey, pumpkin pie, sweet potatoes, or stuffing. After the meal, I picked a fight with Charlie.

"Is that a tall forehead hiding under your hat, or is your hairline receding?" I teased.

"Wrong brother," Charlie said, tugging his Paw Sox—Boston's AAA club—hat lower as he perused the tapes and CDs, hoping to DJ the appropriate mood music for clean-up. "John's losing his hair."

"My hair *is* falling out in great clumps, but this is your genetic destiny too, Chas," my older brother said, good-humoredly running his hand through what remained of his. Actually, with his increasingly tall fore-head, John bore an uncanny resemblance to Nathaniel.

"Is Uncle Charlie bald?" Jeremy stared. He and his three-year-old cousin charged in from the living room where, in sublime compromise, they had decided to play house with swords. Jeremy had dubbed himself Sir Peanut Fearsome while Hannah was Dorothy from the Land of Oz.

"One day he will be," I said, trying for a diplomatic tone of voice.

"Stop!" he said, looking crushed. John roared with laughter, happy to cede the role of chief harasser in our sibling pecking order.

"Grow a mustache." John fingered his own with a twinkle. "Real men have the courage to go bald."

"Odds are you will," I persisted. Wasn't 75 percent of male pattern baldness inherited through the mater-nal grandfather?

"Our grandfather was a cue ball at forty," John said, loading the dishwasher while Nathaniel whimpered in his bouncy seat on the kitchen counter.

"I'm sure that Dr. Mulliken would be happy to of-fer hair transplants," Ted added as he put away the glasses. "Maybe he'll give a family member's discount."

"Hey, quit ganging up." Charlie stopped searching the music collection.

"Oh, we love you no matter how you look," I repri-manded.

"Easy to say: you've got a foot-long braid." Charlie glared. He was angry now.

"Bald is beautiful. It's all in how you wear it," I said.

"Can we just talk about the weather?" Charlie flung the words down and I looked up from the sink, suds drip-ping off my arms, startled. At the same moment, Nathaniel wiggled harder, rocking his bouncy seat closer to the edge of the kitchen counter.

"Hey? What happened to our washing-up music?" Ted prompted.

"Your CDs stink," Charlie said.

"Why are you so upset?" I asked Charlie, who was lifting Nathaniel out of his seat.

"Because," he said slowly and carefully. "I'm not ready to lose my hair."

Baldness seemed like a trivial aspect of aging, no big deal compared to the events of the last four months. The latest development was a delay that no one had expected. At the age of four months, Nathaniel could not hold up his head, something that two- and three-month-old babies typically mastered. The pediatrician's worry shaded into such alarm that I reassured him with much more confidence than I really felt. All the other kids with Apert syndrome held up their heads eventually; at least no one had warned otherwise. But the Early Intervention Program, whose specialists might actually know how to help in this situation, had such a long waiting list that its name was a bad joke. The social worker had called in Nathaniel's name on the day he was born but the flood of babies born in 1990 meant a deluge of babies with special needs, making this safety net as useful as a smoke detector without a battery.

"Make sure you support Natie Mac's head," Ted advised, running through radio stations until he hit on a danceable tune.

Ted swung me around the kitchen. Charlie folded Nathaniel in his arms, stroking his nubbly skull, lingering over the bulge, a pulsating reminder that the operation that was supposed to fix his skull had to be repeated. His brain protruded, stuck out, a lopsided goose egg, the kind that cartoon characters get after being knocked out in a boxing match. Charlie forgave the needling and goose-stepped through the overheated kitchen, sashaying his nephew. He was the kid who had stood up to the play-

ground bullies, whose soft spot for the underdog certi-
fied him as a lifelong Cubs fan. Was it because we had so
doggedly harassed him at home?

"I won't let those brutes tease you," Charlie whispered in Nathaniel's ear, giving him a goofy grin.
Nathaniel smiled and cooed in return.

"You are bald," Charlie informed Nathaniel.
"Not me."

❧

Nathaniel would shape Jeremy's life just as surely
as my brothers had shaped mine. While we joked that
my oldest brother was born to bully, I was born to bluff,
and Charlie was born to bewail, I worried that Jeremy
might be born to bite and dreaded his nursery school
conference. It was 7:30 in the morning, and the mother
who had gone before us, a Harvard fast-tracker, scowled
as she left her appointment.

"I asked if Peter had leadership potential—and get
this," she paused to regain her composure. "The teacher
said that she had *never* thought about it."

Our list of questions did not include the potential
for leadership as much as the possibility of a sociopathic
future. Just that morning, Jeremy had been a whirlwind
of fury, screaming, "Mommy, you are NOT bigger than
the world." Now my knees towered above the table-top.

"I want to share two things about Jeremy," said his
teacher, a well-regarded, nursery school veteran. The conference took place in the rigorously organized classroom,
with the adults perched on tiny chairs at even tinier tables,
surrounded by The Pink Tower blocks, trinomial counting cubes, and globe maps. "First, the biting."

The Biting. Was it a major activity for him, like
block play? I envisioned a daily blood bath, a string of
children tattooed with my son's dental impressions.

"School regulations require that I write a report. Any time a child is bitten, it must be noted in the file. Even if the skin isn't broken." My three-year-old already had a *record*. "I should say it happened fast. He was being teased by the biggest boy in class. While they were in line to go outside, the older boy said that Jeremy looked weird and well . . . Jeremy just bit him."

"So, is it an ongoing problem?" I asked quietly, holding tightly to Ted's hand.

"Oh no," she said, surprised. "Where did you get that idea? I hope you're not worried, because he plays very well with the other children." She showed us irrefutable proof: the check mark in the little box marked "age-appropriate" under "Social Development."

"Really?" I said.

Ted shot me a glance.

"He's a great kid. A delight. The second thing is what I really want to talk about. It's . . . surprising. In all my years teaching, I've rarely seen it this young. But did you know that he's reading?"

Ted and I shook our heads.

She showed us the letter board where he put the red vowels, the blue consonants, the upper and lower case letters together to make words. She demonstrated how he would arrange *cat, mat, sat,* and *hat,* sounding them out and then reading them back.

As she walked us through the rest of the boxes on the report card, my first memory of reading rose to the surface. I was four and had heard *Make Way for Ducklings* so often that I was "reading" it to Mom, when in one magical moment, the black lines on the page merged with the words on my tongue until I stopped, betrayed by the fact that "I-land" got spelled "IS-Land." Although reading was my narcotic and salvation, a three-year-old reader seemed like a dangerous and subversive proposition. It was just one more thing to worry about, one more limit Jeremy had tested, one more way that we would never keep up.

"Can you stop worrying now?" Ted asked as we left.

"Yeah, now we have not one but two atypical children," I replied gloomily.

∞

The downward spiral continued. In December, our car died and then so did Larry Bird—our pet zebra finch, not the basketball star. The mechanic was fixing the car but Jeremy had a hard time understanding why the doctor could not do the same to Larry. Then, flying back on the shuttle from New York City, Ted ate a piece of honeydew melon and in the process somehow managed to swallow a plastic fork tine. When Ted went to the hospital, Jeremy asked, with a child's uncanny logic, if the doctors were going to fix Daddy's head too.

The car's demise meant taking a cab to pick up Ted at the hospital where he had been treated.

"What's wrong with the baby?" the cab driver asked after we squirmed into the back seat, his eyes straying effortlessly over Nathaniel's head and hands.

Everything, I thought.

"Nothing serious, I hope?" he prompted, staring kindly at us in the rearview mirror.

"No," I said, presenting an image of good will. "He's just born like this."

"You don't mind my asking, was it something you ate?"

"No," I said looking out the window at the leafless trees, the tightly packed, nearly identical houses of the neighborhood, boring in their similarity.

"You look like an athlete," he said and then added a little later, "You don't smoke right?"

I shook my head.

"I don't even let people smoke in the cab." He idled at the stoplight. "This has nothing to do with sex, but do you have heavy periods?"

I burst out laughing at this excessively creative attempt to find a rational explanation. "No. He was just born like this."

The cabby paused and then said, "God bless you. Does your husband know how lucky he is being married to you?"

"He does," I said.

"Why is Daddy lucky?" Jeremy whispered in my ear.

"Because he does not have a fork stuck in his throat," I whispered back.

∞

Despite the white Christmas lights circling the front porch, darkness settled in. The endless advertisements that guaranteed happiness with a purchase, the exhortations to make this Christmas a perfect one, merely deepened the sense of failure pervading our house. Jeremy was transfixed by the glittering ribbons and the decorations but confused Santa and God, elves and angels, the North Pole and Heaven. Ted and I debated what Christmas story to tell him when childhood experiences of nature, more than the Episcopal church, had shaped our beliefs about what was sacred and holy. So we decorated the hibiscus tree, a present to Ted fifteen years earlier from his girlfriend who was driving the car in the accident that nearly broke his neck, because it was an emerald reminder that life goes on. Under the tree was a skirt of gifts, but with the exception of the latest edition of the Merck manual that Dad and Jane had inscribed, none that we truly needed.

Dad and Jane came to celebrate the Christmas holiday. Lawyers in the same firm, they worked long hours, especially at the end of the calendar year. Dad, who looked younger than his 65 years, never seemed to flag, perhaps because he maintained constant forward momentum like a fish. But Jane had chronic insomnia, which she handled by reading cookbook recipes in the middle of the night. And when possible, by taking catnaps.

I walked past the guest room and saw Jane flat on her back, arms folded across her chest like a marble body on a sarcophagus, so still that I flinched, afraid suddenly that she had died. Jane was so quiet that people routinely underestimated her power. She had short, gray hair, a porcelain complexion, and the kind of gentle face that belongs to a favorite aunt. But anyone who spent time in Jane's company quickly realized that her assessing eyes missed very little, even closed. Sensing my presence, she sat bolt upright and immediately apologized for neglecting her manners by falling asleep.

"Do you want to go swimming?" I asked, eager for exercise to counteract the inevitable holiday overeating.

"I don't have a bathing suit." Jane hesitated.

"You can borrow one of mine. Can't you?"

A year ago, Jane had had a mastectomy for breast cancer. Breast cancer. The club that many too many women joined. Its ubiquity, familiarity, and treatability softened some of its terror. While her prognosis was excellent and she talked candidly of the weakness in her arm muscles and the inevitable disfigurement, still her loss was in a place too private to share. Jane made a foray to her suitcase and modestly placed a pinkish, gel-filled prosthesis in my hand for inspection.

"What's the worst that happens?" I asked, curious about the faux breast, round as a mushroom cap, complete with lifelike nipple.

"It falls out," she said simply.

Jane smiled but decided to stay home and catch up on sewing her quilt square instead.

∞

One holiday night, sitting on a hard pew in a drafty church in Boston's Back Bay, listening to medieval music, I prayed. I was trying to figure out God's role in all that happened. In Hebrew, Nathaniel's name meant God's gift. But what did that truly mean? Our kind elderly neighbor across the street, who car-pooled with the ladies to Mass every Sunday, said that Nathaniel was a blessing. The baby sitter whom we had shared with our next-door neighbors said resolutely that God never gives you more than you can handle.

Nathaniel's soul, his guardian angels, the feeling of "no big deal" that came out of nowhere at his birth strengthened my faith. But, I wondered, if God wanted Nathaniel to have Apert syndrome, why would she be so mean? And if God never gave people more than they could handle, what about my in-law who had committed suicide? If Apert syndrome was a blessing, why wasn't everyone praying for a kid who had it? Why couldn't God be all powerful and all good at the same time?

As a child, I had believed that God shaped a family. Perhaps that's why I never asked the questions about sex that parents dread. When I first noticed that my next-door neighbor was an only child while my best friend was the youngest of seven, I mulled over these structural inconsistencies, naïve of the carnal facts of life, and came to a holy conclusion.

Eventually, sex elbowed God aside. Instead of a mystical, white-robed man who gave heavenly souls an Earthly address, a school of sperm swam furiously toward the mighty egg until the lucky one nibbled through the zona pellucida and two sets of genes spliced in ecstatic union. But only when the time came to have babies rather than prevent them did I truly appreciate that rational explanations *only go so far*.

For thousands of years, philosophers have sought answers to the question: where do babies come from? The ancient Greeks believed that miniature men—homunculi—resided in the sperm, docking with the egg for nourishment. Even with the advent of the microscope, which made the egg and sperm visible to the human eye, this theory held sway. The first scientists to examine sperm swore that they saw a homunculus. But this theory begat a difficult question: how were the homunculi created in the first place?

Now scientists focus on the gene to explain the mysteries of creation. In fact, genomania gripped the end of the twentieth century. In an extraordinary exercise, scientists had nearly deciphered the genes of the fruit fly, the mouse, the zebrafish, and the nematode worm. The human genome would soon be decoded as well.

While genes do connect parent to offspring, the medical papers reduced Nathaniel to a mutant deformity, a glitch of DNA. The implication that any gene "explained" my son was as ridiculous as making a stone responsible for the great pyramids of Egypt. The facts of life were neither straightforward nor simple. How can the essence of a living creature be explained merely by the molecules of which it is constructed?

It seemed provident to me that the science of genetics was invented by a monk working in his garden, for as surely as space mingles with time, so does the body blend into the soul. In the NOVA video that Ruth's parents had shown us, one schoolchild asked a mother if God had given her son his craniofacial condition. "Nope," she said, not missing a beat. "If God could have made him perfect, God would have. The

syndrome just happened." Ted and I liked that. Shit
happened, even to God.

∞

The year turned, the ground froze hard, and Cambridge turned dull and leaden. Nathaniel, at the age of
five months, still could not hold up his head and we
prayed for intervention in any guise—early, late, secu-
lar, divine. I loved Nathaniel the way he was but could
not imagine either his head or brain staying the way they
were. The operation to fix the steadily increasing bulge
had been delayed because Dr. Mulliken, who usually got
one baby with Apert syndrome each year, had been
swamped with three and nobody knew why. Was it a temporary swell that would be followed by a dearth? Was it
magnetic storms stirred up by the sunspot cycle? The
soup of chemical toxins in the food and water? Legacy of
nuclear fall-out from the Bikini Atoll open-air atomic
testing in the 1950s? A generation that sat too close to
the TV set? Dr. Mulliken and his colleagues would probably never have an answer because these conditions were
just too rare a public health menace for the government
or private industry to fund research.

Worse, Nathaniel didn't even have a pediatric hand
surgeon because we had the luck to live in Boston, where
each of three highly trained specialists wanted exclusive
rights. It would have been less tumultuous to live in—
say—Nebraska, where the only choice worked eleven
hours away. The HMO surgeon, whose youth was more
unnerving than his lack of experience, wanted
Nathaniel's case but we lobbied for the senior doctor with
the national reputation. An appointment with the third
pediatric hand surgeon promised to break the impasse.
But by the time we decided on which of the three would
do the surgery, we had become such specialists on the

hand specialists that the pediatrician relied on us to explain their debates. I grew despondent. So what if I knew my carpals from my tarsals? The fact was that we could never be an expert about our child because no one knew enough to qualify.

Our family pace of life, always lively, accelerated. As a typical child, Nathaniel came along for the ride. (The one exception was a winter vacation where Ted and Jeremy went to the Dominican Republic with my older brother's family while Nathaniel and I went to Florida with Mom and her husband because it seemed imprudent to visit a Third World country with Nathaniel's brain still sticking out of his skull, unprotected.) Jeremy went to nursery school in the mornings but no longer napped in the afternoons. So we took expeditions to the neighborhood restaurant for a treat of cocoa or took public transportation, just for the thrill. We met Ted in Harvard Square for haircuts or went downtown to Boston's Children's Museum, which Jeremy loved. When the snow fell, we dragged plastic sleds to Fresh Pond and slid down the hill, Jeremy screaming with pleasure and Nathaniel in terror as the cold snow flew in our faces. Jeremy built forts in the backyard, rolled tiny balls into huge boulders, and launched snowball fights.

At the end of the day, I read out loud while Jeremy gave his brother a bottle as if he was plugging a hole in a dike. Jeremy was enthralled by knights and dragons, the sagas of Erik the Viking and the Ninja Turtles, and especially the story about a little boy named Alexander who tamed the dragon under his bed by making friends with it.

Mom worried constantly about my energy, but so much needed to be done. We had applied to a progressive elementary school for Jeremy but that meant an interview, which we prayed would include no biting. When our car showed its final signs of mortality, Ted and I bought a new one, a first for us. Nathaniel got hauled along, a scrawny baby with a strange bulge on the side of his head who threw and caught smiles, grabbed things, gurgled, and cooed. But except for a peaceful time in the morning, he often found himself frustrated, his face knotted in rage. Ted and I were tuned into his moods but others found Nathaniel difficult.

He was soon going to be six months old, the age at which Jeremy crawled into mischief and never looked back. All the other babies born in 1990 to our siblings, cousins, and other family members toddled along their merry way, while Nathaniel's head still flopped. Because he could not hold up his head, he relied on us to do what he could not accomplish himself. Blankets bolstered him in the stroller and backpack. Our bodies formed a backrest. He tracked sounds and sights, wove his way through the mighty confusion of his world, but not nearly well enough. Head control is essential when a baby begins to explore the world beyond. To satisfy his growing desires, Nathaniel needed to stabilize the position of his head.

It was getting harder to hold up my own. I had bargained on a child who looked different and would endure an unthinkable round of surgeries, but not one locked in infancy. My equilibrium stemmed from the faith that love helped Nathaniel grow, but this delay in development seeded doubt. Perhaps he was not essentially like other kids after all.

Once worry became established, it propagated like a virus, infecting everything. Now I worried that Nathaniel was mentally retarded. Dr. Mulliken had been careful to say that no reliable data existed on whether or not mental retardation was part of the syndrome. In his opinion, many with Apert grew up mentally retarded because they had been treated as if they were, especially in the past, deprived of medical and educational attention, even institutionalized. The majority of his patients had normal intelligence but he guessed that as many as one-third did not. Although both Ted and I sensed that Nathaniel's cognitive abilities were typical, my worries spiraled out of control. How could we be sure? And if he was mentally retarded, what would that mean?

In *Exceptional Parent*—a magazine for families of children with disabilities to which we now subscribed— I read about a girl who was blind, speechless, nearly immobile with few cognitive functions or hope for improvement. The mother struggled to explain her daughter to wondering strangers and curious friends but the usual explanations failed because they dwelled on "doing." Since "doing" was not what this child was about, she finally settled on saying that her daughter was an angel, a pure spirit come to Earth to teach us the meaning of unconditional love. Could I be capable of that kind of love? Could I dare?

I suspected that I loved Jeremy too much for his accomplishments, for narcissistic validation of Ted's fearless coordination and my encompassing memory. When would Nathaniel hold up his head? The staff administrator at Children's Craniofacial Centre put us in touch with another family whose son with Apert syndrome had taken seven months. But seven months seemed like eternity.

The first sign of progress came in mid-January with a call from the Early Intervention program which felt like the official welcome to Nathaniel as a valued citizen of the Commonwealth of Massachusetts. The plan was that, every Monday, a physical therapist would come to our house for an hour, and every Thursday morning, Nathaniel and I would go to the Early Intervention school in Somerville's Davis Square and join something called Baby Group.

The Cambridge-Somerville Early Intervention program was a pioneer, one of the best in the nation. Still, I hesitated outside its door for the same reason that every child hesitates on the first day of school. Who would be here? Where would we fit in? I missed Ted, aching for the way that his presence balanced out my own tense worries, for the comfort of his experience as a summer counselor at a camp for the blind and deaf, but most of all, for his friendship.

The first floor housed a preschool classroom, painted in primary colors. Beyond the coat cubbies, the main room opened with ample ceilings, a sloping wooden slide, a playhouse, mirrored walls, gymnastic mats, and endless shelves of toys. Only the bright bolsters used to prop up kids lacking muscle strength and control gave away the clientele.

A slender woman with a twinkle in her eyes introduced herself as Bonnie. She was the same physical therapist who had evaluated Nathaniel at the age of two months. Along with a speech therapist, she conducted a formal assessment, put Nathaniel through his paces—laying him on his back and sides and belly—but mostly they watched and took copious notes.

Bonnie politely motioned us to the gymnastic mat at the far end of the room where she had arranged a sampling of toys. When I had asked how she would work with Nathaniel, Bonnie explained that at the core of Early Intervention was the belief that a child's earliest experiences have a lasting impact on his future. By intervening—with information, exercises, stimulation, expertise—at the earliest possible time in a child's life, the trajectory for a child "at risk" can be shifted. The idea seemed so obvious but Bonnie patiently pointed out that there was a waiting list because of funding problems, and there were funding problems because legislators did not buy the thesis of Early Intervention. After all, its intellectual foundation crossed the nature-versus-nurture fault line. Can scientists prove how much of our destiny is scripted by nature? Is the pattern of development so firmly ingrained at birth that nothing can alter it? Are we born *tabula rasa* or *fait accompli*?

With gentle respect, Bonnie plumped Nathaniel on a large orange ball and moved him slowly, back and forth, finding out where his balance gave out and where it was strong. She was not perturbed in the slightest when his head flopped like an addict nodding out.

"Why are his shoulders hunched up to his ears?" I asked.

Bonnie paused, asking herself the same question. "I don't know."

She lay him on his back and dangled a red rattle just within reach, working with a vigilant yet calm confidence. He stretched and with enormous effort, his tiny mitten hands moved toward the ring and his fingers touched and closed as far as they could.

"Why do his eyes track only for a moment and then lose their focus?" I asked, thinking that I sounded like Jeremy, endlessly chiming why.

Bonnie reflected again. "I don't know."

I wished that she did but her unflappable voice carried a sense of wonder and intrigue that suggested Nathaniel was a puzzle to solve together. For the next half hour, Bonnie experimented with what Nathaniel could and could not do until he wailed with fatigue and wiggled to be nursed. When the social worker announced "Circle Time," the other mothers and their children moved off their respective mats into the center of the room. As we slid over, Bonnie whispered quickly, "I think his shoulders are hunched because it takes all of his neck and shoulder muscles to hold up his head. It's partly because his head is big but may also be what we call low tone. That's a descriptive word for muscles that are not particularly quick to respond. Anyone can have low tone. It improves with age, exercise, and usage. He does seem weaker on his left side than the right and I don't know why his eyes lose their focus."

"What can I do?" I asked. The other mothers familiar with the routine sat cross-legged on the floor and flashed hesitant smiles which suggested that either they were pre-occupied or respectful of my privacy.

"Anything to strengthen his shoulder and neck muscles. Place him on his stomach for as long as he'll tolerate. Stretch him over a pillow. Show him his favorite toys."

"Baby push-ups?" I didn't tell her that I had already been making him do them.

She nodded. One child was walking, his legs spread for balance, oversized spectacles perched on a button nose. Another toddler scooted on his knee like D'Artagnan fencing. A baby with a pink hair-bow scowled in her mother's arms. After a feeble round of parent and children singing, everyone lumbered to their feet for snack time. The social worker hauled a heavy divider curtain across the classroom. I must have looked confused because she explained that the therapists would feed the kids on one side of the curtain, while on the other side we had coffee or talked.

In the relative quiet on the adult side of the divider, the fatigue of the last six months mixed with the glow of relief that the wait for Early Intervention had finally ended, that help, even in the form of slightly burnt coffee, was here. At the social worker's request, the mothers seated around the round table introduced themselves. The fashionably dressed woman with an expensive haircut said that her baby—the girl I had seen scowling—had Down syndrome. Next to her, the heavyset woman had the boy who wore glasses—also Down syndrome. The quiet woman was the mother of the scooter with, no surprise, Down syndrome.

Of all "birth defects," Down syndrome qualified as one of the most common. Tomes had been penned, careers built, a prime-time TV show launched, and our HMO had so many families that it had started a monthly support group.

It was my turn. "My name is Jeanne and my son Nathaniel does not have Down syndrome."

They laughed good-humoredly, mocking the sense of placelessness that comes when a child's development is not sheltered under the great umbrella of the bell curve. In the big world and even in this little red schoolhouse, Nathaniel was not an average kid but an outlier, at the map's edge where ships fall off the flat Earth and dragons roam. Suddenly I wished for a child with Down syndrome so he would not be peerless, in a class all by himself.

∞

Despair crept over the boundaries Ted and I had constructed to keep it out. The prolonged stress of waiting—for the next surgery, for Nathaniel to hold up his head—depleted all reserves, making it impossible to believe that there would be a time when everything would be right again. We got shorter and testier with each other. All that remained for me was a zealous but increasingly hollow conviction that we could survive this, while Ted's can-do spirit evaporated, leaving him blue. The waiting threatened to drown us.

"We need help," Ted finally said.

"Another appointment?" I said in disbelief. "I'm maxed out."

"This one's important," he said.

The voice of the NICU social worker, when Nathaniel was a day old, echoed in my ears. "A child like this brings some couples closer together and pulls some couples apart." Through the fog bank of fatigue came the clarity that we had a moral responsibility to pull together, that it would be a sin to compound the strikes against Nathaniel by letting sorrow and perplexity divide us. After meeting with an obtuse psychiatrist who wanted to explore Ted's trauma from the long-ago car accident, we finally found a social worker who counseled rather than analyzed, urging us not to blame but remember that love meant extending each other the freedom to feel differently.

Again, the warning voice of the NICU social worker came back. "Under mad is sad." But sad is a vast polar region and grief particularly numbs the soul, making it hard if not impossible for two grieving people to warm each other. Unable to give the hope lacking within ourselves, Ted and I simply acknowledged that we were in this together, whatever *it* was, the tumult of grief, the universe, life itself. At these lonely moments, the greatest gift was simply to let the other be, not trample on vulnerable places in a rush to avoid being hurt, not blame out of the deep helplessness over events beyond control. It meant practicing the Hippocratic oath to do no harm.

For the most part, the differences in our temperaments complemented each other but sometimes, despite efforts to be gentle, Ted and I got out of synch. The final straw came in the midst of making love. We found ourselves arguing about the conflicting opinions of the three hand surgeons about the risk of operating on Nathaniel's thumbs at the age of six months. It became clear that the very thing we had pledged to avoid had inevitably happened. Nathaniel's syndrome had devoured every sacred normal corner of our lives. From that naked moment on, we banished the medical minutiae to the workday, scheduling phone appointments to discuss Nathaniel's condition and reserving the evenings for the two of us as a couple, to have fun, to be united by something other than strife.

Once a week, a baby sitter came and we went out on a date, usually to a movie but sometimes a basketball game. We both loved the Celtics, although tickets were harder to get than an OR date. In the mid-1980s, the Celtics had elevated basketball to a fine art. As one *Boston Globe* sportswriter noted, the Celtics were to Boston what theatre was to London and opera to Milan. The starting five—Larry Bird, Kevin McHale, Robert Parrish, Danny Ainge, and Dennis Johnson—took the game to championship level almost every night that they played.

Most evenings at the Boston Garden, the only available seats were up so high in the dusty rafters that it was hard to see the players beyond the banners. When Ted got floor-side seats for a game against Boston's arch-rivals, the New York Knicks, it was a big night. Although the starting five had aged—Larry and Kevin had injured themselves beyond rehabilitation, Robert barely ran the court, Danny had been traded, and DJ was retired—Larry's ability to materialize from nowhere and seize the rebound without leaping more than two inches off the floor was still amazing. So was Kevin's spinning and whirling in the low post, his unbelievably long arms making him look like a helicopter trying to take off. But while the players clustered around the coach during a time-out, a woman in a nearby seat declared, "Absolutely I had an amnio. I could not bring a child in the world to suffer."

"We did too. It would not be fair to burden our oldest with a handicapped sibling," intoned her friend nearby.

"We are leaning towards a home-birth," she said. "Where did you have your kids?"

Was she talking to me? No. I scrunched my shoulder.

"At Beth Israel." The conversation penetrated through the cheering din.

"Birth is a natural process," she said. "Doctors intervene as if having babies was a disease."

"Who scored?" Ted nudged.

"Reggie, I think." It was hard to concentrate.

"I was afraid to do a home-birth."

"Well, babies die sometimes. That's a fact."

A home-birth would have been a disaster for us. With his initial breathing difficulties, Nathaniel would have been permanently brain damaged from lack of oxygen. Watch the game, I scolded myself, don't squander this night out.

This time, my gaze fixated not on the pick and rolls, hard fouls or fast breaks, but on the players themselves. With the luxury to inspect and scrutinize at such proximity, I saw for the very first time what unusual bodies these basketball players possessed. The men who scurried on the TV screen were close to seven feet tall, giants who did not have—off the court—the luxury of a "normal" life. They drew gawks, stares, and constant jokes about the weather up there.

And height was only the beginning of the player's anomalies. Patrick Ewing had a prognathous jaw, pronounced maxilla. Kevin McHale had interesting shoulder joints, looked like extra bone on the humerus. Greg Minor, under his shaved head, had a very small occiput at the back of his skull. Reggie Lewis's intraorbital distance was narrow. And Joe Klein was more than extraordinarily tall. Something about the thickness of his features suggested that he either had acromegaencephaly or perhaps a pituitary disorder. Why had I never seen these important details before?

"Three minutes left in the half," Ted said.

Reggie Lewis missed the inbound pass but got the ball again, turned suddenly, and, releasing it off the tips of his long fingers, drilled a three-pointer just at the buzzer. The crowd sprang to its feet, the Celtic's coach primly applauded as he checked the scoreboard, and Ted dug a hopeful elbow in my ribs. He cocked his head, sharing his vision of the future. One row up was a cheering father, arms draped casually across the shoulder of his grinning teenage son who had some kind of syndrome. For a joyful moment, it seemed that the entire world was disabled.

My hockey team is called
the Bruins, Like the Boston
Bruins. I play left wing.
Little body checks are ok.
I skate fast when my coach
yells to me. The rink is
smoother than the pond.

# Chapter Nine

❧

# The Butterfly

February 1991

℘athaniel's second operation took place during a cold snap in February when nothing seemed alive or ever likely to awaken. Familiarity with surgery bred rebellion and disgust with the hospital's well-intentioned efforts to soften the unpalatable truth—cheery nurses, toys dangling off stethoscopes, paintings of Teenage Mutant Ninja Turtles, Barney. I vowed never to commit the pre-op instructions to memory, and that was a feat, given how easily such details stuck in my mind. For his part, Ted vowed never to arrive on time. Every small act of defiance added a measure of comfort.

Brenda, the liaison nurse, welcomed us back with a benevolent smile reserved for regular customers, showing off her newly refurbished command-and-control office.

"Help yourself," she said, pointing to the bowl of M&Ms that gleamed jewel-like on her desk. Ted declined while I popped a clicking handful.

"What's the candy for?" Ted asked.

"When my father was in the hospital, no one wanted to get close to his sickbed," Brenda explained with a conspiratorial air. "Everybody stood at the door, talking across the room but he couldn't hear a word. So I put a bowl of M&Ms by his bed, and suddenly the cousins lined up to hold his hand. Candy keeps the lines of communication open. Surgeons tend not to be, how shall we say, talkative people?"

But they liked sweets. After saying goodbye to Nathaniel in the OR, we had gone downstairs to the cafeteria for breakfast and bumped unexpectedly into Dr. Mulliken, who was washing down his plate of bacon with chocolate milk, a reassuringly nutritious breakfast for the twelve-hour surgery ahead.

We found that the first hour passed at a laggard pace. Although the family waiting area had been renovated, the tension in the air was still so free-floating and remorseless, the dread so infectious, that Ted and I sat in the sunny hallway overlooking the snow banks outside, trying but failing to concentrate.

A couple whose eight-year-old son with Apert syndrome was also having surgery—just tonsils—introduced themselves and stopped to chat, waxing wistfully about the old days. But when they confessed with a whisper that it got harder not easier as the child aged, Ted and I both looked away.

The discipline required to cross-stitch a thumb-nail sized pillow on my quilt square occupied my attention for awhile and then I gave up and began working the *New York Times* crossword. Ted stopped searching through an HMO balance sheet and was just about to call his doctor; this time he had bruised his elbow, ice skating with Jeremy.

He was standing up when a woman screamed, the sound so sharp, primordial, and unexpected that the pencil fell out of my hand. It detonated from a room in the family waiting area, reverberating through the entire third floor of the hospital. It was the saddest, most unforgettable sound I had ever heard and I knew immediately that I never wanted to hear it again. Just when the scream became unbearable, it stopped but the brief silence was soon shattered by another scream, this time louder, higher-pitched, and even more piercing. The acoustical pyrotechnics drilled the walls like deafening jackhammers. There existed no decibel to measure the stranger's lament. Finally, the screams subsided into anguished groans and then faded into gasping breaths.

Ted and I looked at each other knowing instantly what had happened: the one thing that parents fear when a child is born, and then fear again when saying goodbye in the operating room. Ted was frozen and I cried out of relief that it had not happened to us.

Later when the liaison nurse came to give us an update on Nathaniel's progress, I asked the inevitable, "That woman? Did her child die in surgery?"

Brenda held the clipboard like a shield to her chest, set her mouth in a thin line, and nodded sadly. "Her child had been sick for a long time."

"How do you tell people?"

She looked out the window, focusing on the pale distant sky. "Often, I tell them what they already know."

The memory of the woman's screams still rang throughout the family waiting area. Ted, whose warm sanity was buoyed by striving to live in the present, had to escape, to get as far away from the hospital as the beeper allowed. The February air was cruel and cold, scorching any exposed skin, hurting the lung's air sacs. The snow was so dry that it squeaked like sand on a hot beach. Ignoring the arctic wind that blasted across the tall grass of Boston's fens, Ted and I raced each other to the Museum of Fine Arts, fueled by the adrenaline that had been ignited by the stranger's grief.

Inside the building, we rode the sun-dappled escalator, past a Monet Water Lily. A sunny restaurant with white linen tablecloths beckoned. Ted went inside, directing the hostess to seat us at a quiet table in the corner. She ignored our scruffy appearance and handed out tall, leather-bound menus, waiting while Ted and I decided to splurge and indulge, hoping to lose ourselves in a feast of exotic foods—baby salad greens, crab-filled raviolis, warm duck in raspberry sauce, spicy polenta, gorgonzola and walnut salad, cappuccino. The woman's screams rang less.

"It was a wake-up call," Ted said.

"Like the butterflies," I said, as Ted thawed one of my hands inside the tent of his own. Last summer, we had gotten caterpillars in the mail, watched them grow, make cocoons, and hatch. Jeremy and I took one to the back door and set it free. The painted lady butterfly flew about ten feet before a gray mockingbird appeared out of nowhere, swooped down, and ate it. Jeremy chided, "You mean bird." I was astonished and speechless because this split-second lesson in death wasn't what I had planned.

"Like Jane," Ted said soberly.

"Like Jane," I repeated.

Jane now had lung cancer—not a metastasis from the breast, which would have been at least understandable—but a new one that blossomed darkly on its own. It was tough enough to fight cancer once, but twice in two years? And this time facing worse odds. Jane did not deserve this, just when she planned to retire, relax, and enjoy herself. None of us deserved this cruel turn of fate.

I had wished Jane out of my life as a teenager when she had appeared to divide our family but she had earned my deepest love and now I could not imagine how we would manage without her.

"I don't want to waste whatever time we have," Ted said reaching over to hold both of my hands, his intrinsic goodness gleaming. "Why am I cooped up at my desk, tied to the phone? These boys are our best work. And I want to do pottery, garden, and windsurf."

One hour, two hours passed dreaming out loud, painting escapes in more and more lavish terms, sharing ambitions that had little to do with worldly definitions of success until the restaurant emptied and the waiter nudged everyone out. On the way down the escalator, I massaged the back of Ted's shoulders. "Monet painted in his eighties when he was nearly blind."

"Grow old with me," Ted demanded as he turned, his gaze direct and intuitive.

Old for a butterfly was three weeks. How much time belonged to any of us?

But I answered without thinking, "I'll kill you if you die first."

Back at the hospital, the empty waiting room, even when Mom, Jeremy, Charlie, and Trish appeared at supper time, underscored the loneliness of being the last ones left. At 7:30 p.m., Dr. Mulliken finally lumbered out, rubbed his sleepy eyes, and removed his sky-blue surgical bonnet.

"Everything went fine. Nathaniel's fine," he said, cradling the wooden box that held his surgical knives used for the day's sculpting. He launched into a description of the tectonic shifts of bony skull plates, the plates, wires, and screws, the cutting, sewing, patching, pasting. He demonstrated on his own face and responded to confusion about what exactly he meant, by showing us on our own.

"There will still be a small opening in his skull. I did not have enough bone to completely cover it, but that should close up with time. I'm making your brother's head more like yours," he nodded to Jeremy.

Jeremy looked up from the checkerboard with a confused and doubtful expression, trying to puzzle out why on Earth should Nathaniel's head look like his? Didn't the doctor know that everybody was different?

"Would you like a sticker?" Dr. Mulliken asked, reaching into his pocket. "The nurses said I'm not supposed to give out Ninja Turtles. Too violent. How about a happy face?"

"Thanks," Jeremy said shyly.

"When can we see Nathaniel?" I asked.

"About half an hour. Say, what time is it now?"

"8 o'clock," Ted replied.

"Time to eat," yawned Dr. Mulliken. "I'm starved."

"Nothing since breakfast?"

"I snack on hot tamales."

"Mexican food?" He got take-out in a germ-free OR?

"The candies. I eat jellybeans too. But they're cracking down," he said wryly, waving before he headed down the hallway. "Problem with cockroaches or something."

Charlie and Mom filed into the recovery unit first and returned, blank and resigned. When Ted and I entered, the night-black windows mirrored my own sense of desolation. Nathaniel? Is that you? Oh yes! Oh. The sounds escaped slowly from my lips. The shock lay in its absence. The same swollen face, sickly complexion, fluffy turban hiding the ear-to-ear incision, hands swollen like arctic mittens, the cursed vent—only his size had changed since the first operation.

Ted, resting his hands on Nathaniel's face, grew still with a sense of vulnerability. I whispered encouragement in Nathaniel's cotton-plugged ears before they transferred him to the Pavilion Five ICU. Please God. Be kind. On the drive home, the road dissolved into the night. Our own exhausted bodies felt fragile, temporary, and weightless as Ted and I held each other in the empty dark, squirreling strength for what lay ahead. It will not be as bad as last time, we reassured each other, not imagining how it could possibly be.

∾

The next day, the ICU vigil began. After checking on Nathaniel, Ted left reluctantly for work. Missing the easy camaraderie that comes from bucking the same crazy circumstances, I simmered with petulant resentment, wanting him at the hospital every minute, every nanosecond. But after awhile, blaming Ted for his job, especially since it provided health insurance, did not improve Nathaniel's situation. I realized that we needed to be apart sometimes to make it together over the long haul. Division of labor multiplied options.

Mom ran the household but she relaxed about cleaning, food shopping, the laundry, and fielded the same questions again and again—How did the operation go? When will Nathaniel get out of intensive care?—with a more laconic voice than the first time around. She had made friends with our friends, knew which traffic rotaries to avoid as well as the best vistas in intensive care. Since she also believed that success in life was largely a matter of showing up with the right attitude, she drew comfort from her role in making that happen. In the afternoon, Mom collected Jeremy at nursery school and brought him to the ICU's family room along with a present, a book called *Endurance*.

"What a perfect title," I said. "Thanks."

"My favorite," replied Mom, who had collected survival literature since college. "It's about a group of explorers at the turn of the century who set out to cross Antarctica by dogsled and they never make it."

"I can't read it if they die." I blanched at the prospect.

"Oh no no no. The journey is not at all the one they planned. It takes years for them to reach safety. But they do, every single person. It's unbelievable what they endure and even how they come to enjoy it. Now isn't that odd? I remember the feelings but none of the events."

"I'm the opposite. I remember the events," I said, stitching my quilt square.

"Maybe that's the secret of how you survive," she mused with puckish humor.

"Maybe," I said.

Mom was snipping out a row of misplaced X's in her square. "EJ's already done. Should we have given Trish one?" she wondered.

"Not yet," I said, shaking my head.

Jeremy liked the ICU now and passed the time playing Candyland and Chutes and Ladders and hearing the *Wizard of Oz* read out loud. Jeremy also liked Willie, a sassy three-year-old, in the bedspace next to Nathaniel. The bad cold that had sent Willie to the Unit was a reminder that the only thing fragile about life on Earth were the humans who dominated it. Microbes were champion adapters, able to survive in steaming geysers, the frigid depths of the Marianas Trench, and a child's moist lungs.

The nurses respected patient privacy, and as a matter of policy, did not speak about a child's medical condition, but somehow we learned that Willie had been born with an extremely rare condition called prune belly. He had a hole in his throat for his respirator tube, and a go-cart for his equipment because his diaphragm muscle simply did not work, which meant that he could not breathe independently and needed a respirator, a vent, to breathe for him—not for a short stay in intensive care but for the rest of his life.

Jeremy climbed on Willie's bed, unperturbed by the respirator, negotiating the tangle of tubes and hoses as if they were merely a dress-up costume that Willie liked to wear, and they played with Nathaniel's stuffed raccoon. "Willie's my friend," said Jeremy. "Will he learn to talk?"

"He knows how to talk," I said. It was a matter of covering the trach opening with his finger. "But he does not like to talk. It's his way of telling the nurses that he's angry to be here."

Remy was the intensive care nurse in charge of Nathaniel and Willie. She was unsentimental and sardonic, a fifteen-year veteran of the ICU who had taken care of so many kids after craniofacial surgeries that she was shocked to learn how rare the conditions actually were. Remy received the brunt of Willie's anger, which she understood to be as much a part of health as his oxygen saturation levels, but still she welcomed Jeremy's presence. "It's good for Willie. He needs to be with kids his own age. He's in the hospital too much." When she saw that I would neither interfere nor flinch, we divided the work. I washed Nathaniel's face, placed pads over his eyes, and rubbed his back while she measured urine, took blood, and delivered medications. Together, our hands and voices embraced him almost constantly. Remy understood that helping Nathaniel was the way that I helped myself.

The morphine kept Nathaniel free of pain and asleep, thank God. Where would he be without legal narcotics? Every hour, Remy opened the locked drawer next to his crib and counted the vials of morphine assigned to Nathaniel. Every vial had to be tracked and destination accounted for because, like all corners of the Hospital, the Unit had a problem with drug theft.

"Who's stealing?" I asked.

"Last time, it was one of the nurses," said Remy, confirming my worst fears.

"What happened to her?"

Remy lowered her voice, "She got transferred out."
Great, I thought, the nurse is supporting her habit by
working the floors. This was doubly troubling when I
remembered how many pre-med college classmates had
been avid recreational users.

"How are the blood gases?" I changed the subject
as Remy checked the lab print-out.

"OK."

"What's the respirator on?"

"Eight. He had a good night."

"Did he get any more blood?"

"Just about to give it to him now."

Blood splattered on my shirt as she hooked up the
transfusion baggy to his IV.

"Sorry. Take this." Remy handed me a scrub suit
top. I changed, wondering whose blood stained my shirt,
what stranger's red corpuscles carried oxygen in
Nathaniel's veins. Ted and I had donated our blood for
Nathaniel but when his surgery date had gotten abruptly
canceled, a nurse mistakenly gave our blood to some
other child, cruelly taking away one of the few ways that
we could personally, intimately help our son. It was one
of the few times that I completely lost it: I screamed hys-
terically—"You Stole Our Blood!"

Now they had stolen our baby. The ICU intensified
my awareness of the intimate bond that Nathaniel and I
shared. *This is not him!* I wanted to shout when I returned to his cribside, wearing the scrub suit. He's re-
sponsive, happiest in the midst of Jeremy's four-year-
old friends. *These are not his noises!* He wails, cries, hic-
cups, gurgles, and coos, making an endless symphony
that is the music of my day. Even in sleep, his snores and
snorts infiltrate my dreams, seeping so thoroughly into
my subconscious that I wake if he's too silent.

*This is not his skin!* His is so caressable that we are
in constant touch during his waking hours. *This is not*

*his face!* He's got an irresistible smile that shines through his frustrations at not being able to hold up his head. *This is not normal!* He wakes up happy, playing with the toys that Jeremy brings, like a magi, to his crib. He loves Ted's kiss on his plump cheeks before Ted runs to catch the bus. He loves the steamy warmth of a shower. *This wretched place is not ours!*

"How about the Foley? Any news on when that'll come out?" I asked, pointing to the catheter.

"Not yet."

"When was the last time he got morphine?"

"At seven. He's due in another hour."

"The ICU chief come by?"

"Should be here soon. Hey, are you planning on going into medicine?"

"No way," I answered.

The separation required by intensive care drove me to the brink of despair. To have no body contact, to hear none of Nathaniel's myriad sounds, to feel none of his inevitable wetness—all of his normal bodily secretions were measured, analyzed, and sealed away—these were cruel deprivations. My heartache about having Nathaniel in intensive care had prompted a seed of courage to grow. Because it bonded me to my baby, I learned about respirators and catheters. For peace of mind in a world of addicts and ineptitude, I studied hard. Mostly I wanted my prayers to be accurate. I didn't expect God to micromanage the ventilator setting but there was no harm in asking.

∞

Ted settled into the rhythm of the Unit, respecting that intervention dictated its own rules. Forearmed with the knowledge that the decision to extubate would be made by the ICU doctor in consultation with the chief anesthesiologist, he did not press or page Dr. Mulliken but waited exactly 72 hours to the minute to pop the question.

"Not yet," the ICU doctor said.

Nathaniel's lungs were soggy with fluid, the result of a close call during surgery, a bit of information that would have been lost to his thickening medical chart if not for his current status. His blood pressure had plummeted, and to boost it and keep him alive, he had been pumped full of fluid, a life-saving measure that now made breathing on the respirator difficult.

On the fourth day, I asked about extubation.

"Not yet," said the ICU doctor.

Nathaniel had a fever. The portable X-ray machine that rolled up to his bed revealed pneumonia microbes growing on the bottom lobes of each lung. The doctors boosted his IV cocktail of antibiotics, cautioning that the drugs worked only against the bacterial pneumonia, not the viral form.

On the fifth day, Ted and I asked together.

The ICU doctor shook his head.

The microbes dwelling in Nathaniel's tiny alveoli clogged them so badly that they collapsed, making it impossible to cough up the thick glue-like mucus which naturally coats the lungs. Four times a day, the physical therapist tried to do it for him, standing over his tiny body, hands cupped, thumping him like a tribal drum.

The otolaryngologist, known for his Yogi Berra-like malapropisms, came by for a consult. "It's a tough road to hoe" and "The worst is the social stigmata" were my two favorites, but when he said, "We can always give Nathaniel a trach," I failed to see the humor.

I stopped asking about extubation and asked instead how often children died, which was the closest I came to voicing my own fear.

"Hard to say. On average? Once every couple of weeks. But it's been awhile. The last one was Thanksgiving," said Remy. "People in the Unit don't like to talk about it. We work so close to death. You've got to be a little crazy to stay here."

A computer-printed sign by the phone read in big bold letters: Honesty Without Compassion Is Cruelty. ✓

"What was your hardest case?" I asked, thinking that her fifteen-year stint constituted more than a little crazy.

"A preemie, born to two doctors. The mom was a psychiatrist, the dad was an internist. Everything that could be done had been done but the baby just wasn't making it. They screamed at everyone. When it came time to turn the ventilator off, we called in the ethicist and they blamed us all."

By the end of the week, Nathaniel's ribbon scar was well-knit but we were unraveling. The stalemate and inertia of intensive care meant that there was little to do and even less to talk about, except to acknowledge how much hatred the Unit inspired. The small army that had mobilized for the operation chafed on standby alert: Ted cleared his work calendar, Mom filled the freezer for Ferd, who claimed to her doubting ears that he was too old to learn how to cook, Charlie DJ-ed music, grandparents and siblings had a telephone tree, friends blocked out time, church congregations prayed.

At night, Ted insisted on countering the Unit's siege mentality, slogging through the snow and freezing slush to escapist movies in Harvard Square. Jeremy happily received ticklefests, extra books at bedtime, and his favorite macaroni and cheese supper. Grandma Julia was staying so long that she became a permanent fixture with her hiking boots, kimono bathrobe, and favorite brand of shampoo in the guest room closet and her spelt, millet, and vitamins on the kitchen shelf. Jeremy forgot she lived in Chicago or had a husband named Ferd. I spent so much time at the hospital that he called Ted "Mommy."

Ted leaned on me and I leaned on a multitude of friends. Alice called nearly every day with a funny story. Lynnie brought food to the hospital. Nancy sent astral love. Jules cut her aikido seminars short to visit. Peg helped out with Jeremy. Cappy sent boxes of chocolate. Gish and Sandra supplied books. Bob dropped by whenever he was in the neighborhood, which was often. June conferred with the doctors. Margaret dragged me to Harvard's enormous indoor pool to go swimming, and Katherine took the Zen high road with tennis. Smashing a bright fuzzy ball would be therapeutic, perhaps even revelatory. Besides she had already booked a court.

Mom summoned the ancestors, casting out stories of hardship overcome like wish pennies into a fountain, using their voices to augment her own. Her great-grandfather Bela Wellman lost more fortunes than he made before coming penniless to San Francisco with the 1849 Gold Rush and starting a dry goods business. He married the daughter of an abolitionist preacher, made his wife a business partner in an era when women could not own property, and luck turned around. Before long, Bela's ghostly presence was joined by those who survived the Potato Famine, busted prairie sod, crossed the West in Conestogas, sailed around Tierra Del Fuego to the Sandwich Islands, ran stops on the Underground Railroad, farmed the rock-fields of New England, and settled Tasmania.

I read *Endurance* until I was lost in the Antarctic, my sailing ship trapped and destroyed by pack ice even before the dogsled expedition had begun, fighting off attacks by ravenous seals, eating blubber stew, camping for months on ice that split under the tent, trekking across drifting floes. After a year, we took to the most perilous ocean on the planet, the Wedell Sea, and traveled 800 miles in 22-foot-long boats with rocks for ballast. We survived hypothermia, sleeplessness, lack of fresh water, dangerous reefs, and a gigantic rogue wave. Nearly two years after the ice had destroyed our ship, we landed on South Georgia island, forced to traverse the unmapped interior and scale a 10,000-foot peak. We got caught by nightfall at the top of the mountain. The whalers camped on the other side of the island were our only hope for rescue, but they would leave in a few days, not returning for another year. I took a chance and leaped into the void.

The Odyssean proportions of Ernest Shackleton's journey did put the ICU into perspective. At least I was warm and dry, sitting next to Nathaniel's crib, eating chocolate, sewing the quilt, or reading about car crashes, hold-ups, incest, schizophrenia, near-death, death, and celebrity motherhood in junk magazines. I was grateful for the visitors who eased the tedium and broke the ICU's homogeneity, although Cindy was the only one acclimated to the harsh hypnotic environment. For some reason, the Unit made everyone else garrulous. One friend simply ignored the surroundings while another drank in the scenery but both told stories that I had never heard, never suspected of being true: car crashes, hold-ups, incest, schizophrenia, near-death, and death. What else was there to talk about?

One afternoon, Charlie—who brought audio-analgesics, a CD of Venezuelan conch-shell band and a tape of kid's songs for Willie—succumbed to the ICU's confessional spell.

"Do you like Trish?" Charlie asked.

"Yes," I said, distracted by the permanently arched feet of a naked Barbie doll nearby.

"Really?" he asked.

"Yes," I said.

"No, I mean, do you *really* like Trish?" The serious tone diverted my attention from the poor doll's deformities. I stared into Charlie's brown eyes, wondering how to frame my hearty approval.

"Oh, why yes I do," I confirmed with Midwestern understatement, glancing at Ted before adding quickly. "Do you?"

Charlie's eager nod betrayed his joy.

"Is this an announcement?" Ted asked.

"Whoa," Charlie laughed. "Not so fast."

"Oh say it!" I teased.

"M-m-m-m," Charlie played along.

"M-m-marriage," Ted coaxed.

Jeremy scrambled over and leaned his head against my cheek, "Who's getting married?"

"No one," Charlie said quickly.

"Yet." I smiled, grateful for any reason to celebrate, praying that Jeremy would not sing, "First comes love and then comes marriage and then comes the baby in the baby carriage." It had been going around at nursery school.

∾

The first good news appeared in the large plastic bag attached to the foot of the crib. On the ninth day, Nathaniel's output of urine increased. The more he peed, the faster he was clearing the fluid out of his lungs. Remy reduced his morphine and lowered the setting on the vent. But how much longer would he last? Even our baby sitter's amiable attitude toward the vent cracked as Nathaniel's body gave new meaning to the concept of wasting time. The bones in his hands surfaced like logs in a dry marsh. The intravenous fluids could not sustain him more than two weeks. He had already been on them for a week and a half. The vent had to come out so he could eat and drink. The longer he spent on the vent, the harder it would be to wean him off, the greater chance it would scar his trachea. I worried with a panicky catch in my voice. Our baby. Last night, Mat had remarked on one of his night-time chart-reading visits that every day for a week, the doctors had written— "Extubate tomorrow."

"So what's happening?" Ted asked.

"Every day, there's been a new problem," he said, sad but not surprised by how quickly they accumulate. The cloud over Mat's eyes signaled that Nathaniel was in trouble. Every day, some random variable had tipped the balance further out of his favor. Wait and see. Wait and see. On the eleventh day, the ICU doctor finally decided to stop waiting and give it a try. He looked careworn, and, for someone who regularly patrolled the frontiers of established order, worried as he said, "We'd like to have Mom in on a consult."

While they removed the tube, I ducked out to tell Ted of the decision but when I came back, my adrenaline surged so hard that I needed every bit of self-discipline to control the urge to sob. This hammer-bong of emotion was, of course, the very reason that parents were not allowed to be in on procedures.

"We're not giving him morphine," said the ICU doctor. "He needs to be able to breathe on his own. Do you understand?"

I barely nodded.

Nathaniel was bleating, almost inaudibly, too weak to cry, propped upright with his head cocked back to free his tiny airway. His emaciated chest heaved, the intercostal muscles clenching with each painful intake. Five adults—the ICU doctor in charge, Remy who knew Nathaniel's medical responses better than any of us, the respiratory therapist, and two young residents—clustered around the metal crib, soberly focused on the numerology of his breath.

"Not great," said the ICU doctor, shaking his head.

Remy took blood samples from Nathaniel's arterial line, sending them to the ICU's lab for immediate analysis while a resident probed his various pulses, feel-

ing around his wrist, then ankle. The respiratory therapist held a mask spewing broncho-dilating, oxygen-en-
hanced mist near his mouth, while the ICU doctor
scanned the blips on the machine—Nathaniel's oxygen
levels, intakes per minute.

This fragile life always exists in the crucible of terror and possible extinction, Joseph Campbell once
wrote. That is why parents wake a sleeping infant to
check that he is really alive. That was why, for nearly
two weeks, I sat at Nathaniel's bedside. If I could have
breathed for my son, I would have. All I could do was
touch him with my voice.

"You're doing great," I said. "Wake up little guy.
Come on. Cough. Keep going. Don't stop. Breathe,
Nathaniel, breathe. You're going to make it."

The print-out rushed from the lab showed his
carbon dioxide numbers to be discouragingly high. As
much as the lungs need to take in oxygen, they also need
to flush out the body's carbon dioxide waste. Too much
carbon dioxide in the blood meant that Nathaniel would
turn dopey, fade out, and eventually poison himself. He
was listless, but that might be the residual morphine in
his system.

The subtle variations of the ICU doctor's expression, a tightening at the corners of his eyes, told of his
worry. He continued to decipher the real-time monitors
which showed that Nathaniel's inhales per minute inched
up, and then tumbled, without apparent pattern.

"I want to see that rate in the 30s or 40s," said the
ICU doctor. "I can live with it in the 50s for the moment,
but if it stays high for much longer, he will tire himself
out, and the tube will have to go back in. Is this how he
normally breathes?"

Five tense faces veered my way.

"No," I said, wishing that was not the truth.

"How's his position?" asked Remy.

"He'll do better if you can get his head as far back as possible," I said.

Remy carefully took him out of the infant car seat, manuvering the wires. With rolled up blankets to support his back, I cradled his head with one hand and held the mist-mask with the other. One resident took another round of blood gas samples and whisked them off to the lab. The other continued to monitor Nathaniel's pulses, probing for the ebb and flow of his life.

"He's slowing down but not much," she told the ICU doctor tersely.

"Got a lot of goo," said Remy.

"Let's see if we can get him to cough some of it up," said the respiratory therapist.

Nathaniel coughed, frail as a shadow.

"Let him go another half an hour," the ICU doc said.

When the next round of lab results came back, the doctors caucused over numbers and ratios, sorting out the conflicting data which confirmed what they already knew, that he was maintaining but no more. On the razor's edge, no telling which way he would go. Whatever else, God, just don't put that tube back.

On the loudspeaker, the receptionist paged the ICU doctor, who excused himself with a pessimistic shrug.

"You're doing great. That's a boy. Cough. What a fighter," I said.

"The cheerleading helps," said the resident without enthusiasm.

"Lots of junk in there," said the respiratory therapist.

I pleaded, coaxed, urged, encouraged, persuaded, bullied, and wheedled. When I made kissing sounds in his ear, he started to cry and my discipline teetered.

"He's really dopey."

"Time to check the blood gases again," said Remy.

"Shit. We just lost the arterial line," said the resident.

"Figures, right?"

"Always falls out just when you need it."

"Find another vein."

"Can't."

"Down by his ankle?"

"Nope. Shut down."

"We might have gotten enough. Let's send it off."

Who were all of these strangers?

The results came back a third time showing that he had not gotten worse, good news, under the circumstances, but no one smiled. The only acknowledgment was that the ICU doctor called the younger ones away to another bedspace.

"Keep breathing. You're getting stronger," I said.

"I dunno," Remy yawned and checked his wrist pulse against her watch. Nothing new. "We got a full house of kiddos today."

"You mean staff?" I was making conversation.

"No. The bedspaces. Let's hope no school bus flips over."

"What's that like?" I asked.

"Chaos. You don't want to be here."

Willie's alarms went off. "Can you?" she grimaced.

"Sure."

She left me and Nathaniel alone for the first time in nearly two weeks. Every fiber of my being twitched, chest heaved, eyes welled, and knees buckled. If I cry, I'll have to leave. I reached for a stool and remembered to breathe.

"Good job, Nathaniel. You're doing great."

If I cry, he won't hear my voice. My fingers turned white from holding the mask so tight. The wall clock with the sabre hands said that two hours had passed, the eternity in an eyeblink.

"Over the hump, Remy?" I asked. She stood next to me, arms folded across her chest.

"Don't get your hopes up." She snapped, hating to make a prediction.

"Your best guess?"

"He's still working hard." She paused to read the blips again. "Maybe."

"Can you watch him?"

In the family room, I surrendered, feeling like Orpheus when he rescued Eurydice from the underworld with the sweet music of his voice. Now, close to the surface of the Earth, the fear of losing my loved one was so piercing that I closed my welling eyes, knowing that if I looked back, I might lose him forever.

∞

Nathaniel got off the respirator but he did not sleep or eat. He was not strong enough to nurse, so Ted cut a small slit in the plastic nipple and gently squeezed the defrosted breast milk in his mouth. He lay in his oxygen tent, a seven-month-old baby weighing less than twelve pounds, an inconsolable simulacrum of what he had been two weeks earlier. Even though Nathaniel had been drugged for eleven days into a state of semi-oblivion, he had existed in a world of bells, dings, rings, alarms, and constant light. Deep in his primitive and essential core, the Unit had made him crazy—ICU psychosis, in nursing parlance.

Twenty-four hours later, he was transferred to Eight West, where he got stronger and began to nurse but still did not sleep. Nathaniel barnacled himself to my body, so that I lurched around, braiding my hair with one hand, propping Nathaniel on my chest in bed, even taking him to pee in the bathroom. After he had been awake for three days, his eyelids finally started to flutter, a sensation whose associations he fought. His head sagged but then he righted it with a jerk. He lay in bed with his eyes open in the dark.

When at four a.m. Nathaniel dropped off, I promptly did too, into a flat dreamless stupor. Suddenly, a gray-haired doctor, with a herd of doctors-in-training in tow, loomed over the crib, politely coughing while the others thronged closer.

"Neuro-surgery," he identified himself. "How's he doing?"

The clock read 6:15. This twit woke us up after two hours sleep to ask how Nathaniel was doing? Did the doctor have a neurological problem? This place endangered its own experts. Nathaniel peeked at the white-coats and bawled.

"He's been inconsolable," I said flatly.

The gray-hair reflected for a moment and the students crowded in closer so they would hear his weighty words, "Might think about a CAT scan."

I shook my head, and made a split-second decision, like diving under a wave or swerving to avoid a headlong collision, and for the first time in weeks, laughed at the absurdity of it all.

The school bus that I ride on is loud. The motor is relly noisy but the kids are quiet. I talk with my friends. The bus driver plays the radio.

# Chapter Ten

❦

# Spring

April, May, and June 1991

Spring brought celebration. Winter's metallic air lifted, purple finches plundered the greening grass, and daffodils pierced the wet earth, their yellow bonnets quivering in the chilly wind. A month after the second operation, Nathaniel held up his head, a triumph that changed everything. When Nathaniel raised his periscope, his world expanded beyond my breast, his sense of security outgrew the crook of my arms, and he reached gleefully for Ted, who reciprocated with fiery joy.

Ted had loved Nathaniel from the beginning but now that he experienced the intense focus of the baby's adoration, his burden of anxiety dissolved and in its place was a light-heartedness that refreshed the house. He came home at night and scrolled through the odd funny details of his day—over-julienned food served at work lunches, one elderly partner who snored through meetings, a terminally serious pair of colleagues—and then organized family sit-ups. Jeremy served as ballast for the adults and then one of us held Jeremy's feet as he struggled to fold his wiry little body in half. Finally, we all lay eye-to-eye on our bellies, tempting Nathaniel with a plastic brontosaurus, cheering as his arms pushed feebly against the rug, impressed by his new-found strengths yet afraid to relax into complacency because of the work ahead.

In the morning, Ted swept his tie over his shoulder like a horse's tail and gathered Nathaniel in his arms to tour the backyard garden, inspecting the daily progress of the fat hyacinths, climbing roses, the fecund peony, orange-rimmed narcissus, and ghostly white jonquils. Never had New England spring been so colorful, extravagant, and outrageous. Time dissolved in the garden, where the abundance of life and its myriad variations acted as a powerful amnesiac. Ted had a green thumb, a natural way with living things and, inevitably, he picked bouquets to fill the house, arranging the blossoms and leaves with a whimsical aesthetic, selecting just the right-shaped vase, finding just the right location on the dining room table, the kitchen counters, and our bedroom. When the entire house was awash in a floral frenzy, he wrapped a few extra in a small piece of wet towel and covered it with a piece of aluminum foil, to brighten the climate-controlled cubicle in his skyscraper. Often the 7:30 bus lumbered by but he was too busy, too intent on celebrating, to care.

As Nathaniel emerged from his fetal slump, I fell into my own and for the first two weeks of April, barely noticed the riot of flowers around the house. While Nathaniel napped, it was all I could do to perch on a stool and listen to the surviving zebra finch flit around its bamboo cage, twittering like a dot-matrix printer.

The phone rang.

"You sound absolutely exhausted. Are you resting enough? You should nap when Nathaniel does," Mom said, her solicitations counterpointed by the twang of country music in the background of her city apartment.

"It's OK."

"Take plenty of Vitamin C. Five hundred milligrams three times a day— the powder's fine. I don't know how you just keep on going without getting sick."

"It's OK."

"And exercise. You're still swimming and playing tennis, aren't you? The endorphins make a world of difference."

"I am." Friends made my exercise their mission.

"You're such a stoic. You didn't get that from me."

"Stop, Mom," I said finally. It was good advice but that was the problem.

"What?" she said taken aback.

"I'm sad. That's all. I don't want to be fixed." I wanted to simply feel what it had been impossible to feel while Nathaniel was in danger. I did not want to shut her out or fray the trust between us. Mom had become the helpful grandmother that her own grandmother had been to Ganny when EJ was born, but in the process also a more joyful mother than when we had been children. Nathaniel erased her gentle rivalry with Ted for my affection— the small doubt that no man could ever be good enough for her only daughter—even healed old wounds with Dad. With genuine care, she and Jane corresponded, sharing the intricacies of being a grandparent and sewing the quilt-squares.

"I just wanted to help," Mom protested, as the music moaned in the background.

Talking about grief did not lessen its force or alter its purpose. Ted knew better than to try.

"I know," I said softly, hoping to atone for the unintended wound but unable to explain that her love summoned the courage necessary to retreat into mute, insular sorrow. But for the simple reason that we were both mothers who wanted to alleviate a child's suffering and were powerless to do so, this bond was too poignant to acknowledge, much less share.

I hung up, enjoying the embracing silence of the house, even the dust particles that spun like fairy dust in the sunlight. In the bathroom, I turned on the tap in the claw-foot tub and pulled the curtain on the window overlooking the neighbor's house. Last fall's anger toward our neighbor had spent itself, like a summer thunderstorm, and now it seemed funny that she had helped inadvertently, by providing a safe and convenient target for thousands of nameless furies that Ted and I might have unleashed against each other. In the warming weather, we saw more of each other, and Jeremy and Ben played together, although this time, it was Ben who was having trouble controlling his aggressive impulses, acting out scenes of Teenage Mutant Ninja Turtle destruction with theatrical fervor.

From the steam-enveloped tub, I picked out Jeremy's plastic toys—the wind-surfer—his version of Ted's real one—and the stiff-armed man with mitten fingers and a bland face who rode across the waves. I gingerly stepped in, thinking of the ancient ritual of immersion, the watery places where life first began, of Jane too weak from on-going radiation therapy to sail. Dad wasn't even going to put their boat in the water this year. When Dad talked about the progress of Jane's treatment and the latest articles in the cancer journals to which he subscribed, we commiserated about what it meant to be general contractors on a health-care job. Dad's obstinate refusal to yield surged through the phone wires, but the bitter hint in his voice betrayed that Jane's retirement might be permanent. I refused to imagine. At sixty, Jane was too young and vital to die. Drifting into a state of warm torpor, I slipped lower and lower, submerging until my body floated in muffled silence.

∽

Through May, June, and July, through the first two hand operations and countless more that got scheduled and then canceled because Nathaniel had a cold, Baby Group was a lifeline. Ted wished for a comparable place for fathers but there really wasn't any so he had his membership by osmosis. I looked forward to the round table where we periodically met and shared the irreducible elements of our lives. The participants of Baby Group included a business manager at a day-care, student, architect, high school drop-out on welfare, housewife, physician, secretary, nurse, and social worker. Our children had Down syndrome, seizure disorder, holes in the heart, premature birth, deafness, and cerebral palsy. I hated the repeat surgeries, but one mother wished her child had a condition that doctors could fix. I struggled with how to respond to strangers, but another mother wanted her child's condition to be visibly obvious so strangers would understand why she wasn't doing what other six-month-old babies did. I longed for a more common syndrome, but another was troubled by the way that people assumed Down syndrome expressed itself in one way in every person.

It was powerful to simply congregate with other mothers whose babies had special needs, hear the variation in stories, see the experience refracted through the crystal of multiple identities. We talked about the Test several times. One mother wished that she had had amnio or ultrasound because, despite her own suspicions, the obstetrician failed to diagnose Down syndrome until her baby was a week old. Another found out that her baby had Down syndrome from an ultrasound in the eighth month of pregnancy, which helped prepare not only her and her husband but also the obstetrician, who brought a cardiologist into the delivery room. Another flat-out refused any pre-natal test, believing that God decided.

We talked about how there will be genetics tests one day for all of us. Everyone's silent but lurking defects will be discovered and debated. What happens when those in power—employers, schools, insurance companies—have access to the information?

The extremes of our situations made the brutal unsentimental truths about parenthood inescapable. All children arrive without reference, warranty, or money-back guarantee and then bring us face-to-face with the terrible knowledge that once the dice start rolling at the moment of conception, the risks never stop. Children magnify our greatest fears and tiniest flaws, reduce us to the raw rudiments of animal instinct, and force awakenings that are as humbling, painful, and nauseating as those from anesthesia.

Sometimes parents in Baby Group had unrealistic expectations of what the therapists could actually do. One mother railed at Bonnie for not curing her daughter of cerebral palsy, while another insisted that her son could have walked if only Bonnie had purchased a certain piece of equipment. Bonnie was initially shy but I admired her steady approach. She changed a child's developmental trajectory as if steering a supertanker. Her technique was to begin early, move slowly, and watch carefully. Bonnie was also circumspect. She had been working with babies long enough to know that one generation's beliefs about the limits of human nature were irrelevant to the next. There was no magic year, bullet, or anything—just the belief that the most important of all human attributes was flexibility.

Now that Nathaniel held up his head, I noticed how the operations had changed the gestalt of his face. Gone was the dangerous brain bulge. He had a forehead bone and eyebrow ridge which allowed his eyelids to close more completely. He did look more "normal" but I laughed at that observation, knowing that "normal" is whatever you see or do on a regular basis. Besides, Nathaniel's appearance seemed far less important than his rapid and accelerating development.

As Nathaniel's motor control proceeded according to the predicted timetable—progressing down to the shoulders, torso, and arms, fortifying the muscles required for sitting—the fear that he was not essentially like other children receded. With head control came visual stability and with that stability, Nathaniel's personality began to change. As he integrated what he saw with what he felt, touched, heard, and tasted, he became a cheerful, joyous, physically active baby. Bonnie reassured us, with tests and other measures, that his cognitive development was typical. The fears of mental retardation faded.

Bonnie shifted focus to his speech, puzzling that everything came out "Baa" and enlisted Martha, the speech therapist, who observed that the shape and structure of his airway made it tricky to co-ordinate the breathing and tongue movements necessary for each phonetic building block. So did his low muscle tone. Since Nathaniel was a communicative and animated baby who differentiated his intentions—you could feel the meaning in his pointer finger even connected to his mitten—but not the actual sounds he made, Bonnie and Martha suggested signing. That way, they reasoned, his grasp of language, communication, and social development would not be hampered by articulation troubles. Each week, they taught my fingers baby talk that I went home and taught to Ted and Jeremy. It was a brilliant solution that worked: a child whose fingers would never bend—even when they were out of the full-length arm casts needed to protect the skin grafts on his new fingers—

was learning a language of manual dexterity. But if trees and fish spoke with chemicals then surely every hand can dance.

Our sign language had its own family dialect. One sign for "drink" is to form the hand as if holding a cup and tilt the imaginary cup near the mouth. Nathaniel's fingers did not bend, so a hand-tilt near the mouth sufficed as his sign. One sign for "go" is to make a rolling motion with the pointer fingers from each hand. Nathaniel signed "go" with all of his fingers.

Outside Baby Group, I gravitated to Cindy, whose son Torrey was one year old, a sweet child with a striking familial likeness to Nathaniel. The mere fact of Torrey's existence did what no doting parent could ever do. If the odds of having one kid with Apert syndrome were on a par with being hit by a bolt of lightning, then the odds of having two families with two sons, nearly identical ages, within a few miles of each other were outrageous enough that lefties (1 in 10), twins (1 in 80), a step-cousin with schizophrenia (1 in 1,000), and even friend's triplets conceived without fertility drugs (1 in 10,000) looked shockingly commonplace.

Although I was struck by how differently Cindy and I reacted to similar situations, the fact remained that we both had basically healthy children who endured tests, studies, hospital stays, pre-ops, post-ops, NICUs, ICUs, diagnoses, misdiagnoses, no diagnoses, surgeries that succeeded and failed. Together, we struggled with nagging maternal doubts about doing too much and too little, trying for balance between pushiness and vigilance, and sharing intelligence about our common enemy—the inevitable head-swiveling, the nomadic gazing of strangers.

When Cindy came over, we took the kids to a nearby school playground.

"Baa-baa," Nathaniel said. It meant bye-bye, bottle, and backpack.

"Baa-baa?" I asked, touching my back. He grinned and pumped his arms eagerly. The intensity of his emotion, the lack of shaded middle ground between joy and sadness, the constancy of discovery and giddy sense of unbounded possibility, transformed an ordinary walk into a magical event. Even a trip to the supermarket was thrilling. Everything had to be grabbed and explored by mouth or hand and then endlessly examined. Nathaniel stared at the rattle tethered to the backpack, bewitched, losing himself in the colors—RED, BLUE, YELLOW— and then abruptly his curiosity shifted. He looked over my shoulder as I pointed and labeled, sharing his discovery of cars, buses, and trees as if I had never truly seen any of them before. And in a way, I hadn't.

"I force myself to take Torrey to the playground every day," Cindy said as we loaded the boys in the swings and pushed them until they soared through the blue sky. Torrey was her first and only child.

"Why?" I asked.

"I wouldn't go otherwise. I hate the staring," she said. "How do you do it?"

At the moment, I felt a sweet liberation because two "abnormal" kids in public corrupted the whole idea of normality. I didn't respond at first, just slowed the swing down. It seemed like a waste of energy to fight the staring, when, after all, I did it myself.

But the visual loitering was no longer as painful as it had once been. The hurt had first diminished when an athlete scheduled to race in the Boston Marathon stayed at our house. Our friend Alice, who was filming the marathon for a short documentary, asked if we could put Craig Blanchette up for the night. Nike sponsored Craig and featured him in a commercial, lunging for a squash shot, chasing a rebound, zooming around a bicycle track, just doing it—but in a wheelchair. Actually, Craig ambulated whatever way he wished—on stumps, prostheses, in a chair. Twenty-two years earlier, he had been born without legs.

In the morning, Craig thumped out of the guest room, dressed for the day's speed trials in a warm-up suit whose pant legs trailed behind like the train of a bridal gown. Instead of being six feet tall as he had been the night before, he was shorter than Jeremy. Nathaniel beamed at Craig, who was digging into his official pre-race breakfast, a large bowl of unsweetened Cheerios and skim milk. Craig smiled back, looking at Nathaniel's head, the railroad track scar, mitten fingers, with the boldest, longest, hardest, and at the same time, the least stingless stare I had yet encountered. Craig demonstrated that, in its pure uncontaminated form, staring is an utterly harmless but essential act, nothing more than the time required by the brain to process what the eyes have seen.

People need to stare at the unexpected and experience it. Wallace Stegner once wrote that when the first European settlers came to the rim of the Grand Canyon, nothing in their experience prepared them for its utter vastness. Its scale was so beyond their norm that they had no place in their mental circuitry for comprehending it. They did the logical thing and denied its size. Only when they actually hiked down to the bottom did they realize.

The face, like the Grand Canyon, is a natural wonder. But uncommon faces have, by definition, landmarks that fall outside the accustomed parameters. Those whose perceptions have been trained on one landscape initially have a hard time seeing a person with a "different" face. The uncommon face can look alien, even ugly at first until the viewer experiences the person and that alters something deeper in the viewer's psyche and soul.

"You seem so calm," Cindy said enviously.

"Really?" I said wondering how many times my serene appearance, or Ted's unflappable demeanor had been mistaken for the whole picture.

I reflected between pushes, "It is easier having Nathaniel as a second child."

"Why do you say that?"

"With Jeremy, I learned how to be a mom. That was hard enough." I laughed at the memory. No sooner was Jeremy born than the assault of worry began. Danger lurked everywhere: colic, sudden infant death syndrome, an undiagnosed peanut allergy resulting in anaphylactic shock, and paralytic polio from mandatory vaccination. Only as he survived each day and progressed through his developmental milestones—sitting, crawling, walking, talking—did I advance through the less obvious maternal versions of the same. The funny thing was that—objectively speaking—Nathaniel had serious problems but the first time that we left him, I checked that the nearest fire station had oxygen and Ted blithely advised his mom to ring 911 if he turned blue.

"With Nathaniel, I'm learning . . . other stuff," I said as the swings slowed down.

"Like what?" Cindy asked.

As inhabitants of small villages do, we traded gossip about outsiders. I briefed Cindy on my encounter with Mary, a four-year-old at Jeremy's summer camp.

"That baby is weird," she had said at pick-up one day.

"No, he's not," I delivered my standard nonchalant response. "He was just born with a big head."

That usually ended the conversation, but Mary regarded me with a bossy smile. "He's weird."

"Oh no, he's really cute," Jeremy spoke to Mary as if she was the one who had just arrived from a distant galaxy.

"See him smile," I said, expecting capitulation in a few seconds.

"Weird," Mary spat the word contemptuously.

"Hi, sweet little baby Nathaniel," cooed Jeremy's friend.

"His head is tall. It's different, not bad," I said.

Mary stubbornly shook her head, insisting while I kept replying kindly until it was obvious that she was just not getting it. I stood up to leave, ignoring Mary, who followed us to the playground where she hurled the words with an evil sneer. I could not figure out what to do or say. I told Mary to stop, she didn't, and I walked away, sad and defeated.

Cindy related how she had been in a crowded mall, riding the up escalator with Torrey when she caught someone on the adjacent down escalator looking in a way that she did not like. "Quit staring at my kid!" Cindy bellowed across the atrium. The stranger turned and yelled back, "I thought he was CUTE, pyscho-lady!"

The playground emptied out and the shadows of the trees dancing around the red tube-slide caught Nathaniel's attention.

"Everything got dumped on me at once," Cindy sighed. "Did you see that TV segment on teenagers with craniofacial conditions who talked about committing suicide?"

"Typical," I sighed. To the mass media, people with disabilities were victims or demons, objects of terror or charity, heroes who triumphed over adversity, but rarely complicated, imperfect people like everyone else. "Did you see this article written by a psychologist who works with kids with craniofacial conditions? She says that they need four things: a strong, supportive family; a strong supportive community; at least one area to excel in; and a spiritual connection."

"That's what all kids need," Cindy puzzled.

"Surprise, surprise," I said.

After Cindy took Torrey home for his nap, I got Nathaniel ready for his, nursing him in the rocking chair where saffron sunlight streamed through the dormer, remembering how nursing was the only thing that mat-

tered to me those first days after his birth in the NICU.
With three coaches to analyze and strategize, the first
time had not been a private moment between madonna
and child. To my surprise, the goal was not to feed him—
that would come later, one coach reassured—but to teach
him how to coordinate the intricate motions of latching,
suckling, and breathing so that he did not desat. Desat?
Lose his oxygen, translated another coach. I was terrified. How will I know? I asked. He'll turn blue, she said.
Blue blue? No, a pale purply blue, like when you get cold.
Momentarily, I had wished for a color chip to hold next
to his cheek. But as soon as Nathaniel had rooted for the
breast, the NICU's incessant noise, the little monkeys in
the isolette spaceships, had ceased to exist.

I stroked his sloping cheek, feeling the heat on his
skin and downy blond hair, nagged by the thought that
I had not helped Cindy much. It was more than
Nathaniel being the second, although Jeremy made an
enormous difference. At age four, Jeremy's growing
consciousness of the complicated ways in which appearance was reality stripped away the illusion that
Nathaniel's struggles would be unique. When Jeremy
came home from nursery school in the morning, he got
naked and jumped on the couch, as if shedding the heavy
social lessons that the garments held within their
threads. He was proud of being a big boy but sensitive
and so keenly aware of other's perceptions that he threw
his nursery school class picture into the garbage can,
furious to be seated in the front row with the "little
kids." One afternoon at the hospital, he snuck into
Nathaniel's baby-sized car seat, trying it on for size but
when Dr. Mulliken came into the room, Jeremy burst
sharply into tears. "Dr. Jellybean was laughing at me!"
he wailed. "He thought I was a baby!"

Cute was for girls, Jeremy declared with mild scorn
as he positioned himself on the fierce end of the emo-

tional spectrum. His heart's desire was to be what children are not—big and powerful. So quite sensibly, he dressed for the part. For his first dental check-up, Jeremy armed himself with sword and shield, both of which he brandished when the dentist walked into the room. On the way to school, he bunched his fingers into a fist and talked with great agitation about the bullies on the playground, the "cryfaces," and the gangs, none of which were obvious to his teachers or us. At home, he was fascinated by the news of the Gulf War, flipping through magazines, staring at pictures of exploding bombs, asking endless questions about the bully in the desert, declaring, "I'm glad they are fighting. If I was a warrior, I would destroy the bully."

Jeremy's desire to destroy bullies echoed our own. But what was the best way to fight back? Ted and I found the Gulf War grotesque in part because we hated the social lies that war required. He had prepared to file as a conscientious objector during Viet Nam and my book on biological warfare had been prompted by the insanity that science brought to global strife. And I winced every time the television commentators talked about the Gulf War's surgical strikes, as if the OR was not messy, chaotic, and bloody too.

Nathaniel was a good match for our family. Because he had a public persona, like a movie star or a politician, I was his press agent, handler, and security guard. For a girl who had idolized Joan of Arc and Amelia Earhart, I relished the dividends that visibility paid. No one forgot us. I found myself drawn to small neighborhood shops instead of large supermarkets, to family-run businesses instead of chain-stores, to the places where the butcher, the pharmacist, postal clerk, restaurant-owner, barber, dry-cleaner, even the gas-station attendant checked up on how their little buddy was doing.

No one ever called us saints or martyrs to our faces but it bothered me when I heard indirectly that others had. Those words seemed pretentious and out of touch with the simpler reality that the sacrifices required by all children bring adults closer to that which is sacred, holy, and true. When I prayed for a world where appearance was not so important, I was also praying for a world that valued the human spirit.

In reality, the danger had evaporated from the routine orbits. The kids at Jeremy's nursery school no longer magnetized at drop-off and pick-up, asking questions. And Nathaniel had subtly changed our routines. We watched *Star Trek* on TV, comforted by a universe of characters whose facial landmarks created new norms. Despite the loneliness and isolation that accompany rarity, the syndrome had the paradoxical effect of dissolving social boundaries.

Out of the routine, social situations were harder to predict but people advanced more often than retreated, the fascination outweighing fear. With Jeremy, I had learned that babies, like dogs, invite conversation, especially from strangers. But when strangers hesitated with Nathaniel, I became more gregarious and outgoing, deflecting awkwardness by extending delight in my baby. "He's cute, isn't he?" I said gently to the tired young woman on the bus who was stealing looks at Nathaniel. It was my way of acknowledging that her stare was natural but also a cue. Nathaniel, who sat splay-legged in my lap, took pleasure in initiating social conversations, reveling in his own evocative powers. He smiled at her. "Why, you are a little cutie, aren't you?" said the stranger, smiling back.

The world could be an ugly place but I took initiative and crossed that chasm with unbridled optimism that it didn't have to be. Life was too short to nurse animosity or register blame. I played games with myself, betting how quickly I could win a convert. It helped immeasurably that Nathaniel had his own radiant vitality, a beaming smile, and angelic aura.

These rules of engagement became habits so ingrained that in time I forgot that I ever had to learn them. On a typical day, strangers introduced themselves. "I couldn't help but notice what a wonderful boy you have," said a woman in the park. "I'm an occupational therapist," a stranger introduced himself on the street. At the circus, the vendor insisted on giving us free hot dogs. The man who pumped our gas often put in an extra dollar's worth. At the airport, an elderly couple watched me showing Nathaniel the airplanes and then told me about their granddaughter, who had been born with a seizure syndrome. The elderly sought us out, as did people who had any connection to a child with special needs, spilling out stories, taking the time to smile, make a connection. Nathaniel got so many freebies that Jeremy came to believe that this was how the world really operated.

I was calm because people learn. Mary's four-year-old brain was already a very sophisticated bundle of neurons. Like all creatures that move, her brain integrated the information gathered by her senses, making an unconscious, instantaneous judgment to guide her navigation. There was no stopping the neurotransmitters from firing across the synapses in Mary's little cerebral cortex. Her task was to keep moving, to see more than the obvious fact that a face is different, to learn the tolerance and acceptance necessary to survive in the twenty-first century.

I was calm for another reason. After nearly a year of getting lost in unexpected places, the syndrome had ceased to be a trackless wilderness for me. Nathaniel was getting stronger by the day but I was weakened by the calcium and nutrients flowing out of my bones to build his. What is it about a sleeping baby that mothers love? The fabric of my shirt sleeve left a soft impression on his cheek. I watched him breathe, struck by the cycle of loss and gain that constitutes parenthood. Nathaniel slept, one arm limp and dangling, a milk drop beaded on pink lips furtively sucking a phantom breast.

A week later, while Charlie and Trish took care of the children, Ted and I slipped away to a bed and breakfast in the country, to sleep, canoe, ride bikes, and soak, together, in a steaming tub.

We have a pet bird. His
Name is Wayne, after
Wayne Gretzy, the hocky
player. He is a cockatiel.
He can not fly cus his
wings are clipped. We give
him a bath every day
in the sink.

# Chapter Eleven

❧

# $\mathscr{B}$eauty

July and August 1991

Once I visited a magician for an article that I was writing on vision. With a classic old card trick, he taught me that the only way to understand how we see is to realize how much we don't. He shuffled the deck and fanned.

"Pick one," he said. "Write your initials on the card and then slide it back in the deck."

My eyes assiduously followed every movement of the magician's hand.

"I promise you that my hand is not faster than the eye. You are taken in by magic because you know the way that the world is supposed to work. You see not what's there but what you expect to see."

He promptly produced my card and explained: Magic is a collaboration between the tricker and the tricked. I had "seen" him replace the card in the deck when in fact he had not. He created the illusion by laying the visual groundwork, by urging my brain with every clue in his power to jump to an erroneous conclusion. The sleight of his hand created the sleight of my brain.

Children perform magic by coaxing adults to forget what they come to expect, even to believe the impossible. A year after the first dismal trudge to Children's, we carried a radiantly happy one-year-old who, despite the awful surgeries, harbored no grudges. He liked the place: doctors, nurses, even the toys on the stethoscopes. Without the nagging weight of memory, Nathaniel lived in the present, imbued with the faith possible when there is no need to search for reason. We tried to do the same.

A festive air of reunion marked Nathaniel's checkup, which took place, not in Dr. Mulliken's office, but in a conference room in front of a chalkboard and a large attentive audience.

"How're you doing, young fellow?" Dr. Mulliken's chair glided over to Nathaniel, who stopped squirming on Ted's knee and grinned, drooling on the cuff of Dr. Mulliken's white jacket.

"The other day, someone asked if I had a family and I said oh yes, I've got kids, lots of them," he laughed easily and motioned for a tissue.

"What about the back of Nathaniel's head?" Ted asked, ready to get down to business. Those in the far corners stood up with an air of expectancy while others craned necks and leaned forward to observe Dr. Mulliken's technique.

"Hmmm," mused Dr. Mulliken, cupping the palms of his hands around Nathaniel's head with a reckless abandon, reminiscent of Julia Child demonstrating the art of French cuisine.

"Yes?" he lifted his eyebrows, turning to his long-standing collaborators. Their heads bobbed in slow, tentative agreement.

"He needs it," Dr. Mulliken said decisively.

When the surgery had first been broached, I was gung-ho while Ted was circumspect. Now Ted was inclined while I wavered, a see-saw reflected among the team. The insular world for families affected by craniofacial conditions was even smaller for the specialists who met at international conferences to debate the merits of screws and wires, argue about timing, and periodically question whether or not they should operate at all, especially with Apert syndrome when the bones sometimes—ungratefully—grew back to their original positions. Was Nathaniel one of those kids whose genetic code would cancel whatever the surgeons did?

"Tell me again why," I asked, thinking that Nathaniel's forehead already showed signs of crumpling.

Dr. Mulliken frowned, bored by the little boxes of logic that medicine periodically required.

"The human skull is composed of bony plates," he said with a lecture-giving tone. "At birth, the plates typically 'float,' which enables the newborn's skull to compress as it travels down the birth canal. It also lets the brain triple in size during the first year of life. But gradually, these plates grow together. By the age of two, they fuse along suture lines. In Nathaniel's case, three of the skull's sutures—the saggital, lamboidal, and coronal—fused prematurely, in utero."

He gently traced the lines on Nathaniel's scalp, absorbed in thought.

"I've never seen a case with three fused sutures. It would make sense to release—to open up—the sutures in the back of his head, but it is a difficult operation." Dr. Mulliken quickly glanced at his distinguished Korean visitors in the back row and, in response to the interpreter's lifted palm, spoke up. "And one that we do not do very often."

The butterflies in my stomach rioted, hearing a specialist of the not-very-often actually voice those words.

Dr. Mulliken's voice once again swelled enthusiastic and eager, betraying the fun that he had as a craniofacial surgeon. "The brain's mission to grow has forced the bones of his skull to grow upward. The surgery would give his head a rounder shape."

"You mean the operation would be for aesthetics?" I asked.

My gaze darted skeptically to Ted, who shook his head in gloomy disbelief. As a rationale, aesthetics was too slippery, elusive, and weak. It defied measurement in angstroms, cubits, or yards, eluded the confines of definition, changed prolifically from generation to culture to artform. When I was seven, Mom had gone to a formal dance, wearing a gorgeous purple satin gown whose skirt was shaped like an inverted Dutch tulip. It looked ridiculous now. By the end of the twentieth century, the deacons of American style did not consider tall heads to be beautiful but Incan royalty once did. They wrapped and bound the heads of their newborns, using cloth, helmets, and other contraptions during the first three months of life, forcing the soft, pliable bones into a tall, conical shape. In ancient Crete, Cyprus, Egypt, Polynesia, and Greece, as well as among Native American tribes—from the Kwakiutl to the Navajo—parents also shaped the heads of their infants from birth. But these and other interventions to achieve ideals of beauty—lip plates, ear-lobe stretching, feet-binding, Japanese women who surgically removed the epicanthic folds from their eyes to look more Caucasian, pop singer Michael Jackson who erased not only his African ancestry but the manliness from his face, Southern Californians who nipped and tucked away the inevitable signs of age as a matter of routine—seemed not just misguided but verging on mutilation.

"No, no, no," Dr. Mulliken hastened to reply. "The operation would be to help his brain grow. I wish I could tell you what to expect but I've never seen this degree of fusion before."

Ted suggested helpfully, "Maybe someone else has."

∽

We traveled to New York City for a second opinion. The entire metropolis specialized in the not-very-often. With eight million people who stared but never for long, the city was notorious for its facial diversity. Salvador Dali, with his theatrical cape, walking stick, and waxed mustache striding out of the Plaza Hotel, had attracted no more, no less attention than the middle-aged woman at the bakery counter near one of the construction sites where I worked; she had a gray Afro, piercing eyes, and a full beard and mustache.

What was beautiful when each generation distinguished itself from the one before by stretching the limits? No attempt to tackle this formidable question deserved more ridicule for its pomposity than the "Beauty Map of the British Isles" concocted by Francis Galton, the nineteenth century founder of eugenics. He passed women in the street, rated them—attractive, indifferent, and repulsive—and then recorded his data back home by placing pins in a map. (By the way, the Center of Beauty, he concluded, was London.)

Scientists idealized the body into static components when, in truth, it is in perpetual motion. Because the face moves nonstop—with micro-second expressions so fleeting that only a video-camera can record them—it attracts the most nuanced looking. Salvadore Dali and the woman in the bakery were compelling because of the self-acceptance that they emanated, an attitude more powerful and lasting than any physical change a doctor could make.

As the car sped past the Bronx's blank high-rises, New York City loomed dark and sprawling. The landmarks—the Triborough Bridge, garbage scows plodding up the East River, Roosevelt Island's tram—looked familiar. But the city felt as disorienting and foreboding to me as it must have been to my grandmother at the turn of the century. In 1905 and 1906, horses pulled taxis, the White Wings collected trash, and Ganny lived in a Manhattan boarding house.

It had been the last stop in a transient childhood during which her family moved up and down the East Coast while Ganny's father managed the finances of a company that manufactured dried milk. Although Mark Twain—Samuel Clemens actually—was an investor who championed the new product as the answer to India's famine as well as his wife's ailments, dried milk proved ahead of its time. Ganny's father was personable and gregarious but ill-equipped for the demands of a fledgling startup. He ran up debt until Clemens sued and called him a thief. Ganny remembered none of the acrimony, only the night that the celebrated author with the bushy hair, the immaculate white suit, and wild grin came to dinner.

After Ganny moved back to Berkeley in the aftermath of the great San Francisco earthquake, her heart never left again. She grew up in a small town, whose social activities centered on church, school, books, and the Town and Gown Club. Surrounded by aunts, uncles, cousins, and grandparents, she knew everybody and everybody knew their place, making our more fluid way of life incomprehensible.

In time, Ganny became a matriarch and her house the still point around which many families spun. Once a year, our family boarded the train for a visit. For two solid days, we rode through placid fields of corn, wheat, and soybeans until the Rockies leaped to the sky, and then my heart jumped too as I recognized the geological equivalent of someone my own age. The train threaded over, under, and through the massif, descending only when it reached the Golden State, whose desiccated brown hills sent my mother into a rapture that I would never understand.

At the Berkeley station, we disembarked, bodies stiff from sleeping upright because private compartments were an unaffordable luxury, and besides, half the fun came from making cross-country friends in the dome car. Ganny drove us home, marveling at the technology of transportation that had sprung up in her century—trains, cars, planes, spaceships—but she disapproved of the distances that separated families, the silly speed at which modern life rushed by. The gas gauge in her car never registered less than half full, a sign of her eternal prudence. Ganny's house stepped into the hillside with a tiny view of San Francisco Bay and the Golden Gate which stretched like a festive circus tent across the horizon. It had no basement, no grassy yard, just a Japanese garden and a sloping driveway where my brothers, cousins, and I raced flexies—Flexible Flyers like sleds back in Chicago but with wheels instead of runners.

In the spring, during a hiatus between operations, I had taken Nathaniel to California. Ganny's house still provided an anchor, although my plane transected the continent in hours and Ganny was showing the accumulated frailties of ninety-five years. The complexities of Nathaniel's odyssey were more than she could or wanted to absorb. Arthritis crooked the knuckles around her wedding ring and she told many of the same stories, including the one about Mark Twain, punctuated with "oh my" and "dearie." Her world had shrunk as it does with age and she had the shell of loneliness that accrues to the hardiest survivors.

But family was the business of women, home the place from which it was run, and despite the creep of years, Ganny remained in charge. When Mom, Aunt EJ, and Aunt Ruthie whirled around with too many directives, the flint crept into Ganny's voice and that was the cue to retreat. We took a hike in the nearby park where the eucalyptus trees dripped rainbow-colored strips of bark and the neighbor once saw a naked man playing a flute, just like Pan. I carried Nathaniel in the backpack while Mom and Jeremy held hands and all of us puffed and panted, bent double by the steep hill. Above the treeline, a glorious view of San Francisco Bay spread, like a magic carpet, at our feet.

Back home, Ganny occupied the porch chair by the lemon bush and she caressed Nathaniel's cheek with a tender hint of judgment. It was not the disappointment she expressed when correcting my slumped teenaged posture, nor the moral outrage in the anarchic 1960s and 70s when grandchildren defied ladylike and gentlemanly dress with beards, shaggy locks, and armpit hair. (She never did say what made hair so offensive—its abundance or unruliness.) My grandmother had a strong sense of order. She had been a girl who had organized her dolls by height, who had ripped out the sewing in her sampler when the stitches were messy. Only the innocent or foolhardy got Ganny started on what the great unwashed hordes of "Beserkley" did to her lovely town in the 1960s. When I was thirteen, she had marched me down Telegraph Avenue, lecturing on its evils, furious about the social revolution initiated there. The hippies, homeless, and hair-covered—whom she lumped together—got the brunt but she also targeted homeowners who failed to prune, sweep the sidewalk, or tidy the toys in the driveway. In her ladylike way, she attacked those who did not care about appearance because her sense of a safe, secure, and stable world, her social order, depended on it.

I looked out the car window as Ted pulled up to New York University's Medical Center. On the threshold of the hospital, I came out of my reverie, knowing that the operation had nothing to do with vanity, everything to do with the inescapable fact that humans are social animals. I would never make the mistake of thinking that appearance was banal if a grizzly bear had mauled my eyes or cancer had taken my nose. In the realm of the spirit, appearance does not matter. But in the material world, it does. When syndromes, cancer, or accidents alter the face's known latitudes and thwart the certainty of belonging that everyone needs, the individual can choose what to do. We were just in the difficult position of making that decision for a baby.

The New York City craniofacial specialists had a more solemn, formal manner than their Boston counterparts. Not only did their hospital cafeteria have separate sections for doctors, staff, and patients, but they inspected Nathaniel's X-rays, charts, and Nathaniel himself with a competitive air before dismissing us to debate the pros and cons behind closed doors. After three hours, the team's senior doctor delivered the verdict over a highly polished antique desk.

"Often in Apert syndrome, we see one suture fused, sometimes two, but rarely three." He was professorial, his gaze assessing.

"Nathaniel is unusual. We recommend the back-of-the-head operation," he said with a blend of measure and empathy.

"That was the unanimous agreement of your group?" I asked bluntly.

"No," he shook his head, bemused. "You might be interested to know that some of the younger doctors spoke against it."

"Why?" I asked, ignoring Ted's signal to cool it.

"Because it is not easy to do."

At least, I thought, they agree on that.

After Ted peppered the doctor with questions, he was ready but I held back, tormented by the possibility of making the wrong decision. How could I live with myself if something went wrong? How could Nathaniel?

Ted was comfortable with the sketchy information that made medicine an art but I needed the science and there was very little. Even though every major science-driven innovation—micro-surgery, transplants, bio-compatible materials, advanced artificial life support, real-time monitoring devices, diagnostic imaging, powerful pain medication—had transformed Nathaniel's short life, medicine was inexact. Its practitioners worked with people—not noiseless signals, frictionless planes, or perfect vacuums.

And everybody, not just Nathaniel, *was* different. When medicine fleshed out statistical patterns, predicting what might happen to one on the basis of what has happened to larger numbers, it was very powerful. But these doctors were trapped by what can be known about an individual in a finite lifetime, trapped by the pioneering nature of their work. Mostly, they were caught by the Cartesian logic that simultaneously powered and limited Western thought. Rene Descartes, the French philosopher credited with saying, "I think, therefore I am," helped launch the Western belief that the body and mind are two separate entities, which in turn led modern doctors to practice medicine as if the body were a mechanism that could be rationally explained.

So in the end, the seeds of my conviction grew from a story. While the team discussed its recommendation, the friendly clinic coordinator had chatted about a young man with Apert syndrome who played Bach on the piano, no problem, and how awful—parents who had been told, just last week, when their baby with Apert syndrome was born at a major metropolitan hospital that the child should be institutionalized.

"We have a patient here, a young man with Apert syndrome," the clinic coordinator confided. "He was born in Connecticut to a devout Russian Orthodox family. The parents brought him to the clinic when he was a baby and we explained what could be done. They thanked us and said, "We love him the way he is. This is how God made him." They refused surgery for the skull, even to separate his fingers. Love would be enough."

She did not change her expression, just dropped her voice. "It wasn't, of course. The day that boy turned eighteen, he showed up in clinic, clearly having had a tough time. As soon as he was legally able to sign a consent, he made his own choice."

We left New York City. By the time the car crossed the churning waters of Hell's Gate, following the green sign for New England, Ted and I made the choice that we thought Nathaniel would make too.

∞

A sense of control can only be temporary and this one vanished at the last minute when the go-ahead for the operation hung on the outcome of an X-ray. During surgery, Nathaniel would lie on his stomach, chin supported and neck arched like a diver making a swan dive, but if the vertebrae in his neck were fused—as some with the syndrome had—the operation would be delayed, even canceled.

Only a century after the Victorians modestly covered piano legs, hid themselves under layers of garments at the public beach, the human body had been stripped of many mysteries. On the second floor of Children's Hospital, the latest and greatest peeping Tom equipment resided behind lead-lined doors, in vast temperature-controlled suites. At one time or another, we had been pilgrims at every shrine—the CAT scan room, where life-size photos of Larry Bird and Kevin McHale flanked the icy-white machine; the MRI room with its detailed list of metal objects banished from the machine's proximity because of interference with the high power magnet; the cozy, high-resolution ultrasound room where babies bawled; the warren for ordinary X-rays.

Such was the expense of the equipment, one administrator confided, the hospital was obligated to use them around the clock just to recoup the investment. Such was their power that these computerized machines were regarded as bigger prima donnas than the most temperamental surgeons. The technicians worked efficiently, accustomed to the wiggle factor, barking instructions, slapping weighty aprons over vulnerable parts, immobilizing children with a friendly vise-like grip. Click. Zap. Done.

While the film was being developed, I floated in the hallway, showing Nathaniel the paintings of Elmo, Ernie, and Bert and the X-rays confirming the vast wasteland inside Barbie and G.I. Joe. It was getting tougher to distract Nathaniel, to turn these hospital visits into a fun game when he had a stronger sense of his own desires, a clearer awareness of his actions.

Dr. Mulliken strolled by with an unexpected present—a reprint from the *Journal of Reconstructive Surgery,* detailing the first use of the computer in the advancement of the skull's frontal bone. There was an eerie CAT scan picture of Nathaniel, recognizable only to those who knew him intimately.

"Thank you," I said, proud of Nathaniel's small contribution to the literature and intrigued by the fact that my child's internal structures had been visual-ized more fully than my own. I looked up inquiringly for a clue.

"Yes," said Dr. Mulliken, with a benign air of distraction. "We're on."

∞

We survive by making endless small choices that separate the fear of pain from pain itself. When the third head operation took place in the legato month of August, Ted and I took refuge in the garden whose artifice was meant to conceal Nature's violence. The carefully composed landscape, the grassy sanctuary located between the hospital's archipelago of buildings, welcomed everyone—the walkers and sprawlers, the bandaged and bereaved. Ted and I found an out-of-the way bench.

Nearby sat a mother and her two-year-old wearing hospital pjs. Trying to get her attention, he implored "Mama!," but she did not respond. He whined again and again, yanking her arm. When she lit a cigarette, he jumped up and down, yelling louder. He tried yanking her cigarette but she brushed him away, never looking him in the eyes. Undeterred, he leaned up and slapped her on the face. She looked at him and slapped him back, hard enough so that he knew she meant business but not so hard that he cried. In the bitter moment when the disappointed child gave up, I turned to Ted.

"I can't sit here anymore," I said. The pain was too close, the invisible web of suffering too sticky.

"OK," he nodded, understanding. "I need to call my doctor about this sciatica anyway."

"You know that every time Nathaniel goes in for surgery, you call your doctor about some ailment?" I gently teased.

He laughed, "She noticed that pattern too. Apparently it's in my chart that we're having a stressful year. Her staff was wondering if I was a hypochondriac."

❦

That evening, when the operation was over, Dr. Mulliken brought the neurosurgeon to debrief in the Unit.

"That's good. His spokes are moving." The neurosurgeon meant that Nathaniel could move his arms and legs.

"We'll watch for any increase in his intracranial pressure. That happens sometimes when you move the brain. We moved his quite a bit." The neurosurgeon was trying to keep his voice detached, but the pitch and clip to his words betrayed the thrill of pushing the envelope and even Dr. Mulliken's demeanor suggested that they had done something that had not quite been done before.

"How do you move a brain?" I asked, wondering if it was like a piano, apt to go out of tune.

"Very, very slowly," the neurosurgeon laughed. Instead of slouching next to the crib with a stony post-game face, he acted adrenaline-high.

"So," Ted prompted.

"My biggest concern is leak of CSF—cerebrospinal fluid," he said guardedly. "I patched the holes in his dura but . . . ."

Nathaniel's dura was like a phone friend: I felt on intimate terms despite the fact that we had never met. The dura was the tough membrane that covered the brain, the heavy duty Saran Wrap around the jello.

"Sewed one very big area above the left eye," said Dr. Mulliken. The dura was not technically speaking his responsibility, but he was the leader of the expedition.

"How do WE watch for that?" Ted asked.

"Look at his nostrils. A CSF leak shows up first—usually—as clear fluid, dripping from the nose," Dr. Mulliken replied.

"If his nose drips that means he either has a cold or a hole in his head," Ted summed up.

"Yes. A hole in his DURA," corrected the neurosurgeon, asserting himself.

Head. Dura. Whatever, I thought. This wasn't our native language.

∾

Remy caught us up on the latest news after the doctors left. Willie was back home in New Hampshire doing fine, ripping out his vent connection whenever he could, and then she oohed and aahed over Nathaniel, marveling over his sedated body in the way that only someone who works in intensive care can. He looked great! So big! Only five months ago! Seemed like yesterday! Next to the Baggie of shorn-off hair, Ted taped a picture of what Nathaniel really looked like—gleefully astride his scooter truck, with wild blond curls, steering with double arm casts, the same flourescent yellow used by Departments of Transportation for safety vests.

"Good," said Jeremy when he realized that Nathaniel was sleeping in intensive care. His mind was divided about his baby brother. He happily slept on a mattress in Nathaniel's room, climbed into his crib every morning to read and play but he also got furious when Nathaniel knocked over his block airplanes and Lego machines. When Ted put the tape player at the bottom of the crib and played the now memorized orchestral side of "Beauty and the Beast," I thought of Wade Bogg's superstitious habit of eating chicken before every Red Sox game.

∾

In a universe circumscribed by pain, certain idio-
syncratic ideas prevail, one of which was that intensive
care was easy. And it was, as long as we performed with
superficial lucidity, doing only what was absolutely necessary. On the second night of Nathaniel's stay in the
Unit, Ted and I ducked out for a few hours to have supper at his once-a-year office party, held at the Dedham
Country and Polo Club, a place in the suburbs with no
horses in sight. Even though the Club's kitchen specialized in watery corn and over-mayonnaised coleslaw, the
food tasted better than the offerings in the hospital cafeteria. I was such a frequent customer there that the cash-
ier offered me the employee discount.

The boss and his wife greeted us nervously.

"Is it okay to talk about Nathaniel? It must be so
hard. How is he?" the wife asked.

"He's in intensive care right now," Ted said brightly.

She looked stricken, not having heard the latest.
"Is he . . . all right?"

"Yes, he's fine," I said.

"Not really," Ted expanded helpfully. "He's just
had another craniofacial surgery, this time on the back
of his head."

The boss came back from his refill, looking pale.

"He's conked out on morphine," I said, thinking
how embarrassing the truth can be. "We'll go back after
we get a bite."

They nodded, concerned, uncomfortable.

"It is nice to get out of the hospital for a stretch,"
Ted said.

"I'm sure," said the wife.

"Well," said the boss, taking a gulp of his drink.
"Thank you for, er, coming."

∞

Nathaniel set a new speed record, shifting from Eight West on the third day, easily extubated because the operation had been on the back of his head, instead of the front. On the morning of the fifth day, a bright-eyed resident planted a stethoscope on Nathaniel's expanding chest. "Did you hear that Gorbachev resigned? And Hurricane Bob is coming up the coast!"

I shook my sleepy head. World politics and the weather seemed insignificant at the moment.

He looked disappointed. "Once those stitches come out, he can be discharged."

In the treatment room, Nathaniel sat quietly while the resident snipped the black threads.

"Isn't his head great?" the resident asked.

The speed of healing was mind-boggling. Blinking back sleep, I slowly recognized him as one of Dr. Mulliken's pilot fish. "You were there in the OR, weren't you?"

He nodded excitedly. "For most of it. Dr. Mulliken did an amazing job."

"Yeah," I agreed, half-heartedly. There were limits on what I wanted to know. Nancy once told me about a mother who inadvertently glimpsed photographs taken of her child during craniofacial surgery, images so traumatic that she literally went blind for six weeks.

"What do you mean?" He was outraged.

"I feel very lucky to have Dr. Mulliken," I said, not wishing to seem ungrateful but hoping that he would hurry so we could get home before the hurricane hit.

"I've seen what other plastic surgeons do." His tone suggested unnatural disasters.

"Really?"

"Your little guy looks incredible," he argued. "Dr. Mulliken is an artist. No one even comes close."

His endorsement was reassuring. Like the Brooklyn Bridge, the Panama Canal, and Eiffel Tower, the operation was an amazing feat of engineering, but I was galled by the resident's preening pride and pernicious assumption that surgery inevitably made Nathaniel beautiful.

"I don't get too attached to how he looks," I said evenly.

"Oh, come on," he cajoled in disbelief.

"He will look different in six months," I promised, shaking my head.

Nathaniel was discharged shortly before the Governor of Massachusetts declared a state-wide emergency in anticipation of the destructive force of eighty-mile-an-hour winds. The metropolitan area came to a standstill, businesses shut down, public transportation stopped, and Boston's hospitals fired up emergency generators. Half an hour before the roads closed, Ted swung into the entrance of Children's Hospital. Torrents of rain struck the slick pavement in explosive bursts, and roaring winds buffeted the car back to Cambridge.

The hurricane struck and then abruptly veered out to sea. By early afternoon, the neighborhood emerged from shelter to take stock of broken branches, felled wires, flooded basements, cracked windows, smashed roofs, and power outages. Ted, Charlie, and Jeremy played in the streets where the rainwater flowed like a river, splashing in the waves.

"I am so glad to be home." I smiled as Mom snapped the camera.

She grinned. "When Nathaniel was born, I thought you would never be happy again. Today you look like that picture on the log."

∾

With ardent pleasure, we threw ourselves into planning Nathaniel's first birthday, determined to reclaim the normalcy denied. It would be Nathaniel's coming-out celebration, a time to rejoice. The party became our goal, just as single-mindedly pursued as escaping the hospital had been. Early August carried a sparking hint of fall air, a glimpse of summer's ending. When we walked to the toy store, Jeremy peddled his training-wheel bike, pretending to be astride a mounted steed and Nathaniel rode in the backpack, standing on the frame, tugging on my hair when he wanted me to stop. He was conscious of people's differences now, playing with how far he could go to get what he wanted.

Inside the store, Jeremy went straight to the wooden trains, which he pushed around the track while Nathaniel watched, mesmerized by his brother's genius at Making Things Go. He wanted to do everything that Jeremy did. What present to get Nathaniel? I wondered. Because this simple question came on the heels of so many difficult ones, I dawdled in the store, entertaining the colorful possibilities. A busy box? Stacking cups? Why not both?

At home, we cooked a huge sheet cake. Jeremy measured the sugar and spun the buttercream frosting while Ted wrote "Happy First Birthday, Natie Mac" on top. While Nathaniel played with pots and pans, we decorated the house with balloons and streamers. The heat of the day lingered into the night. We ate supper at the backyard picnic table, listening to the crickets sing. There were no words to describe what the year had meant. Nothing made much sense—and the very wish to have things make sense seemed funny. Why should the pieces of life fit neatly together? Nathaniel wore only a diaper but ate with such gusto that he was soon covered in avocado and sweet potato. Jeremy smeared food across his own cheeks in sibling solidarity. I put a sweet potato dot on Ted's nose. Nathaniel giggled and we all joined in.

Our happiness survived three days. Under the backyard hemlock, Nathaniel made heroic attempts to blow out the candles on his birthday cake, oblivious to the cere-

brospinal fluid that quivered in a soft pouch under the
skin right between his eyes. The dural patch had failed,
an emergency so serious that an operation was scheduled
immediately. Without the blessing of preparation, the bol-
stering of routine, Jeremy threw a major tantrum in the
supermarket demanding a Three Musketeers at the check-
out, kicking and screaming on the floor. "When you are
dead, I will eat candy whenever I want."

Mom had commitments in Chicago, Mat was doing
a rotation in Hartford, and hardest of all, we agreed that
Ted should take Jeremy to his mother's house. I was be-
reft by these absences and deeply grateful for friends who
came, but in the holding area of the OR when one surgeon compassionately said that he understood how I felt,
it took every ounce of self-control not to spit in his face.
What is there to understand about pain?

At the end of the day, the neurosurgeon slouched
into the waiting area with a wintry face and explained
his plan to treat Nathaniel's dura like the tube inside a
bicycle tire. Because he suspected that the pressure of
Nathaniel's CSF was making the patch blow, Nathaniel's
pressure would be artificially lowered with a needle inserted between the vertebrae in the small of his back. It
functioned as a drain but carried a risk of infection by
very nasty microbes, which could, like meningitis, attack the meninges or lining of the brain, leaving a child
deaf, blind, or paralyzed. And that was the good news.

"We'll be monitoring his blood. At the first suspicious sign, the drain comes out. It comes out anyway after five days. That's when—statistically speaking—the
chance of infection gets too risky. We can put another
one in. As far as risk, the clock gets reset with each new
drain," he said.

"So the longer the drain stays in, the more the dura
is likely to heal. But the longer the drain stays in, the
more likely he is to get a vicious bug," I said.

The neurosurgeon nodded. "We'll be watching, of course."

The drain was a diabolical device: easily dislodged and something that could only be reinserted under local anesthesia. Nathaniel had to be kept flat on his back and totally inert, a Promethean task. Endless hours passed in a blur of toys, waving rattles, books, twisty things, bright spinning objects, but Nathaniel cried, wiggled, and the first drain fell out before the dura healed. By the time Ted and Jeremy returned from Long Island, the second drain had fallen out and Nathaniel was moved to Nine North, the Neuroward where children had hydrocephalus, seizure disorders, and nameless brain ailments. A fourteen-year-old girl with carrot-red hair and freckles screamed at random, recognized none of her family, and tried to escape at every opportunity. She had been fine until she dove into a swimming pool and hit her head on the bottom.

When Nathaniel's blood showed signs of an incipient infection, the doctors descended like a SWAT team, searching for meningitis. After ten devastating minutes, they concluded it was a false positive. But something else was perplexing so they did a lumbar puncture, which revealed that Nathaniel had destructively high CSF pressures. He needed a shunt now, a permanent drain implanted inside his brain to prevent permanent damage to the most vital organ of the body. But the shunt gave no guarantee that the dura would heal.

Hearing the news, I drew the curtain that surrounded the crib and sobbed into a pillow, absurdly aware that I had not even said hello to the parents of the little boy who shared this room, the only non-neurological case on the floor. His urinary tract opening was at the base of his penis, rather than the tip, and he was our second roommate with this condition. All my life, I had never even known that hypospadias existed and now it felt as common as pigeons.

That night, at Ted's urging, I did what had never seemed possible and slept at home. On the way in the next morning, I fought with the cab driver who had been thirty-five years on the job and citing chapter and verse, informed him indignantly that at seven-thirty a.m. on a Thursday in August, my route was fastest and his was plain wrong.

Outside the hospital's revolving doors, Ted and I passed two couples having heated exchanges.

"Why don't we?" I asked, remembering an ugly fight before one of the hand surgeries when Ted said he didn't want to go. I got all wound up, he had said. Although he apologized and did go, the fight was disturbing and signaled how close to emotional bankruptcy these operations put us.

"Maybe we don't want to waste what little energy we have," Ted said quietly.

On the way in, I bypassed the pennies in my change purse and lobbed quarters into the wishing well, praying for Nathaniel's dura to heal.

∾

One last drain, one last chance. In the white space of the afternoon, the residents clogged the nurse's station, clutching styrofoam coffee cups, looking as if they needed bed rest more than the patients, waiting for the senior doctors to make rounds. The phone rang. My friend Alice had a favor to ask. For a documentary on traditional Chinese medicine, she planned to film brain surgery that relied on acupuncture anesthesia but needed to know—quickly—the name of the pain-relieving drugs that Americans use for the same operation.

Daisy, one of many residents who had taken a turn caring for Nathaniel, answered so rotely that I asked her as an afterthought, "Would you like acupuncture anesthesia if you were having brain surgery?"

Imagining the pain that one can endure is a game that survivalists play. But it was also a distraction from the wrenching possibility that the shunt might not allow the hole in Nathaniel's dura to heal.

She shook her head. "Knock me out."

"Even if someone proved scientifically that acupuncture was safer?"

Anesthesia was, after all, the most dangerous, least understood part of surgery. When the first anesthetics were discovered in the West over a hundred years ago, the experts claimed that women needed more than men, the rich and educated more than the poor and illiterate, and children none at all. Even forty years ago at Children's, senior doctors taught the residents that children felt no pain because their nervous systems were "underdeveloped." And yet, a thousand years ago, the Chinese had invented a safer alternative, a completely different form of pain relief, based on the unity of mind and body, the immaterial but real force known as Chi.

"Who would want to hear the sound of the saw cutting through your skull?" Daisy dismissed the inanely logical notion with a wan smile.

I slouched on a chair in the hallway and contemplated the same choice. Awake or asleep? It was like the game children play—if you had to surrender one sense, which would you rather be—deaf or blind? Deep down, I knew that you simply do whatever you must but the pain that was the hospital's franchise, its raison d'être, seemed inescapable and the choices beyond imagination.

∾

The last drain fell out, shunt surgery was scheduled, and once the nurse soberly disconnected Nathaniel's IV, he went from being cranky and inconsolable to a sociable, good-natured one-year-old with an astonishing appetite for life. He was everywhere, cruising, crawling, swaying, wobbling, sparkling, as relentlessly self-righting as a gyroscope, never looking back, proof that babies are more unpredictable than the weather or the stock market.

Nathaniel led the way, first to intensive care where Remy didn't recognize him upright, then to Ming who screamed constantly, and next to Adam who was celebrating his birthday in the playroom. Frosting smeared Adam's puffy cheeks and his mother hugged him tight although the nurses said that she was beginning to disengage, a good sign. Adam was too sick for a liver transplant and would not leave the floor where he had spent his short life.

In the lobby, we sprawled across the couches, ignoring the pharmaceutical salesmen who worked the phones with the same hustle tactics as their illegal counterparts. Nathaniel felt at home in the familiar surroundings, pulling himself to stand, steadying himself on knees, creeping along the cushions. His attention swam from the wishing fountain to the glass elevator, from the tropical fish tank to the giraffe sculpture. He waved to a passersby, who exclaimed, "What a cute kid! What a bright little guy!" Dura, shmura. With incomprehensible exuberance, he grinned and paid no attention to the Ace bandage that Dr. Mulliken had wrapped swami-style around his head, muttering that it would apply a little pressure, maybe help, couldn't hurt. Like a celestial body, Nathaniel had an albedo, reflecting more light than he absorbed, transmitting the simple joy of being a child across the dark, depressing expanse of Nine North.

"My daughter has taken a shine to your son," said a woman.

"I know her," I said. "She's the one who looks so beautiful without her hair."

"Please tell Kelly that," her mother replied. "We're in Room 908."

Later, I knocked, my hesitations about strangers long gone. Kelly's mother invited us in. Kelly was twelve, with a round face, penetrating blue eyes. While she and Nathaniel played peekaboo, her mother explained that Kelly came for monthly radiation to treat a growth in her brain. She did not use the word cancer, or talk about whether her daughter would be okay. Those details were neither taboo nor relevant because something more important, more wonderful happened. The present crowded out the past and silenced the future until time halted, the material world crumbled, and the miracles or tragedies ahead ceased to matter.

The labor of pain gave birth to the vision that it was quite enough to be, right here. Suddenly the little room expanded until it seemed big and spacious and I was filled with a melodious sensation of surrender. I became very quiet. What was important was the light, its particles and waves, the golden aura that informed the room, the shimmering sun on the patchwork quilt that Kelly had brought from home, the imperial radiance in Kelly's and Nathaniel's eyes.

When four lives crossed for an hour, in Room 908, one afternoon, I thought at first that I had found tranquillity, but in truth, it found me. Two children emancipated a clairvoyance: beauty is the fearless faith in the great mystery of life, the breath-taking exaltation of being alive.

∞

It was too late to be civil or polite to the delegation of doctors hovering nervously by the door when Nathaniel was scheduled for a shunt very early the next morning. The consents had already been signed.

"We like to get input on difficult cases," the chief neurologist said, as my startled eyes flickered to and fro.

"Someone suggested that Nathaniel's elevated CSF pressures are caused by the Ace bandage. We would like to repeat the test again."

The Ace bandage that was supposed to be helping?

"OK," I said. He could have identified the culprit as the dura fairy. "May I stay with Nathaniel?"

Daisy was doing the poking and probing involved in the test but she balked. "Why?"

"To comfort him." Knowing that she probably didn't remember, I added. "I've seen you work before."

She shook her head, preferring no audience, afraid of the powerlessness evoked by pain—mine, Nathaniel's, and most of all, her own.

I paced the hall, dodging the ever-present man with the vacuum cleaner, engaged in the eternal unwinnable fight against microbes.

Daisy emerged, eyebrows arched in surprise. "I'm not supposed to tell you."

The chief materialized at my elbow, beaming, "Good news! Nathaniel's pressure is entirely normal. Surgery is canceled."

"He doesn't have hydrocephalus?" I needed to hear the words again.

"No, he does not. You can go home."

This year, we are Learning about maps. We Learned about Longitude and Latitude but I Like doing my stery powders in science better. Reading is hard work for me.

# Chapter Twelve

❦

# 𝒟own the Stream

*September 1991–June 1992*

"Who wouldn't have pulled through? Every time Nathaniel opened his eyes, one of you was there staring back with adoration," Mom said.

In the fall, Jeremy started his new school, where his four-year-old classmates stared at Nathaniel's bald pate, angry zipper scar, and the Ace bandage to which Ted had added an orange feather for panache. When all was said and done, we believed that the Ace bandage helped but no one would ever know the truth. The kids at Jeremy's school asked a few questions, forgot the answers, and moved on to the more important job of playing. Jeremy himself paid attention to new details—drawing an anatomically correct picture of the males in our family for Back to School Night, and begging for a Mohawk haircut, like the teenagers in Harvard Square.

But mainly he concluded that bodies were made for rough-housing. He confided his ambitions for the future to Nathaniel. "When you grow up, we can both tickle Mommy and Daddy."

As September slid into October, Nathaniel shredded the knees of his pants by commando-crawling everywhere. Now he explored things that he had never noticed before: tabletops, inside cabinets, under the beds. He ventured often from my side, coming back only to share in the delight of his discoveries or his tears when things did not go as he had hoped.

Bonnie's evaluation revealed that his social, cognitive, and verbal development were right on target but that he had physical delays related to his bony structure. As Dr. Mulliken had predicted, by virtue of the brain's plasticity, Nathaniel was a typical kid. Every week, the scar tissue on his dura got 10 percent stronger, so eight weeks after leaving the hospital, when the surgeon's patch reached 80 percent of its strength, it finally seemed safe to believe that it would hold. But returning to Children's for a routine check-up, my hands trembled on the steering wheel until I became convinced that Nathaniel's forehead bulged with a pocket of CSF fluid. Except for this post-traumatic stress flashback, everything was fine and Dr. Mulliken shook his head, perplexed, saying, "Maybe your generation will understand what these fluctuating CSF pressures mean."

The terror receded. But after being ceaselessly vigilant, scrutinizing every little variation in Nathaniel's physical body, worrying what it might signify, the safety felt alien. But in time, other traumas succeeded Nathaniel's operations. Jeremy got a splinter in his finger one day and screamed like a lunatic, terrified by the needle.

That fall, our youth ended and the middle phase of our lives began with a strength tempered by the burdens that a child forces his parents to carry. Nathaniel injected a sense of urgency about what mattered and what would last, simplifying many complexities of family life. Once Ted and I had struggled with the legacy of our parents' failures, the ghosts of who we thought the other should be. My greatest fear then was that our differences would prove too great. Now it was impossible to imagine how we would have survived the last year without them. No one completely understands the workings of another person's soul, but Ted and I would never give up trying and this tenacity helped us preserve the contagious madness of love at a time when others drifted apart. In the trial-and-error experiment of marriage, in the many second chances that a long-term relationship allows, our souls had blended. The symbiosis was permanent, inextricable, and mysterious. Ted worried about events that struck without warning while I ignored them; he deliberated while I acted on impulse. We fought less to convince the other, knowing that the truth was not in objective facts but the richness of dialogue. What became important were the moments shared, the simple act of listening, accepting without judgment or rancor, trying to love what is because nothing else exists.

I didn't realize how many extraneous layers had been stripped away nor the heady freedom that loss can bring until one day I went swimming at the health club and, after laps, stepped into the pool-side shower, where I peeled off my suit and goggles. Soaking under a hot thundering spray, I was filled with unexpected joy. I turned off the tap and stepped out of the shower. For a couple of minutes, I lingered by the picture windows that opened into the busy weight training room, equipped with machines and barbells, watching the heavy loads that people lift by choice. Bending down for the towel, I realized that my bathing suit was still hanging in the shower. The funny thing was that being naked in a public place held no shame. Aware that people see only what they expect to see, my mistake felt so laughably human.

∞

At Christmas, Dad was subdued by the melancholy awareness that everything with Jane was happening for the last time. She danced no more jigs in our kitchen. Instead, she moved slowly, getting winded from climbing the stairs to the second floor, unloading the dishwasher, even casually conversing. Her already thin body was frail, her porcelain skin was waxy, and behind her eyes lay an abiding fatigue. Although Jane was delighted that Charlie and Trish planned to move into our downstairs apartment in the spring, she fretted about her unfinished quilt-square, the house still under construction by the lake, how Dad would manage alone. Dad's face was drawn, his shoulders stooped, but he played gallantly with the grandchildren. "I think that Jeremy reminds your father of himself as a child," Jane observed quietly.

This time, Jane made no apology for taking a nap and instead of the prosthesis, she mentioned another hidden disfigurement, the tiny tatoo on her chest required to align the radiation beam that was supposed to destroy the lung tumor. But that was all Jane shared about her medical treatment. She had stepped into a finite universe, which meant that time spent on the subject of death had to be subtracted from what little remained.

Between Jane and the children, who acted as if they had all the time in the world, the only safe place to be at Christmas was the here and now. There was no swimming, no brisk walking in the dry cold air, no medieval music, just the unblemished happiness of watching Nathaniel lurch, teeter, and collapse as he took his first steps within the protected circle of family.

Nathaniel's walking marked the distances that our species had traveled in a million years. The intensive parental care required by all babies in the first year of life was a legacy from the past when our hominid ancestors stopped loping across African savannahs on their knuckles and stood on two feet. The bio-mechanics of upright posture constrained the size of the pelvic opening, which meant that the earliest Homo sapiens babies were born before they were fully developed, when their heads were still small and plastic enough to pass through a narrow birth canal. Human babies really have a gestation period of twenty-one months—nine months in utero and the first twelve months outside their mother's body.

Nathaniel's standing also marked the distances that Jane had traveled. The joy on her face contrasted to her reactions during her first NICU visit, when she had apologized for getting in the way, when each piece of information that we found comforting made her shrink and whiten. Instead of bubbling with hope that Nathaniel was breathing and nursing, she had been grief-stricken by the colossal feats he had to accomplish.

Now it was our turn to make the adjustments that love demands. Jane possessed grace which, as Edith Wharton wrote, was what you need in the dance of life when you don't know the steps. But what happens after the music stops? Haunted by Jane's approaching death and the mystical vision that came unbidden in Room 908, I attended Quaker Meeting.

Some things require silent waiting to see. I had glimpsed divine beauty in Room 908 and it had struck me dumb. God's presence filled the noiseless meeting house. There was nothing solitary about this silence. I sat quietly and balanced my love of science with faith in the mysteries that reason will never penetrate, knowing with bittersweet clarity that just as the body intermingles with the soul, so do the things that can be explained merge with those that cannot.

And I caught a tangential glimpse of what lay ahead for Jane in the memory of a sailing trip across Lake Michigan. Becalmed in the middle of the vast inland sea, under a cloudless indigo sky with nothing but watery horizon in all directions, Dad cast out the sea anchor. We jumped into the lake. Jane, frightened of the water, was the last to leap. I splashed and paddled, aware of being a human speck in the immense blue, awed by the depths below and the incomprehensible infinitude above. Now I wondered why we must locate our love for people within the temporary vehicle of a body. Hers would be gone soon, and try as I might, I could not imagine how to contact her without it.

∾

The year turned once again. Like all babies, Nathaniel did not stay little forever. By January, he toddled along, became contentious and in reckless enthusiasm, broke things, learning that if he banged too hard, his toy hammer snapped in two. If he stepped on Jeremy's Lego machines by mistake, he could make his brother scream.

As his miraculous veneer wore away, we had the sweetest privilege of taking him for granted. In January, Nathaniel had his last hand surgery, the final operation, at least for the time being. Ted totaled it up: four craniectomies, three syndactyly releases, four above-the-elbow casts, five stays in intensive care, 75 hours of anesthesia in the operating room, over 500 stitches, ten units of transfused blood. And in some inexplicable way, the numbers added up to the child that everyone had forecast. He was a great kid.

In the spring, our two-family house blended into one when Charlie and Trish moved into the downstairs apartment. Love was in the timbre of Charlie's voice as he taught Jeremy the words to a Jonathan Richman song: "I was born by the Fenway at Beth Israel Hospital. Could that help to explain why I love the Fenway so well? Nowhere do I feel more at home it seems than on the Fenway where I dream my dreams."

By June, Larry Bird retired from being a professional basketball player, the college students decamped from Cambridge, and we did too, taking a river trip in Utah, where the unrelenting sun obliterated the shadows cast by the last two years. I had never rafted before but my brother John, who lived in New Mexico and had navigated the San Juan six or seven times, mockingly called it "the kid's river." That label conjured languid water, pastoral tranquillity, a riffle here, a ripple there. To everyone's surprise, it had been a snowy winter, which meant a big spring run-off, which meant in turn that the river roared with standing waves that curled back in sneers. The speed of the current prohibited even sturdy children from wading at its edges and Ted, who harbored hopes of kayaking, gave up after his first Eskimo roll in the gelid waters.

While we perched like grim gargoyles on a mountain of waterproof gear bags and boxes, John demonstrated how to steer from the center seat with his oars pointed out like shotguns, how to read eddies and swirls, to travel at an angle, pull away from danger, and pick the flow that you want. Ted took the pilot seat next while Mom scouted anxiously for rocks, Jeremy and his cousin Hannah screeched gleefully with each jostle, and I cradled Nathaniel, wondering what on Earth were we doing here? What silly notion had possessed us? For five days, thirteen people—nine adults and four children under the age of five—would hurtle down this hydro highway? What if the rafts tipped over? Even with a life-vest, Nathaniel was too little to get his head out of water. Wasn't the river too frigid for him to last long before hypothermia set in? What about an emergency? Five days at the bottom of a steep gorge, with no living soul on the mesa above, except the occasional shepherd tending a flock of sheep, no hospitals within hundreds of miles? I couldn't decide if we had crossed the line from adventurous to stupid.

It did not take long to figure out that the river was in charge and we were merely passengers, going along for the ride. By the second day, when my fears subsided enough to try steering, I was enchanted and mesmerized by the beauty of the river as it snaked through desert land, past cliffs that buckled like an enormous car in a tragic crash. Under a cloudless sky, the only movement in the landscape came from the sun's transit and the muddy river itself. Or so it seemed at first.

Pilgrims and visionaries retreat to the desert for revelation because its scale of earthly trauma dwarfs our own. These rocks moved but not at a rate that was humanly comprehensible. The sandstones, mudstones, and limestones layered like a deli sandwich were the sediments that had been buried, exposed, buried, and exposed in an impossible to remember sequence. Uplifts! Upwarps! Orogenies! Geologists liked to say—I wouldn't have seen it if I didn't believe it. It took a giant leap of faith to imagine that the arid desert was once a warm inland sea.

But it was. I loved the planet's inconstancy, the power and ubiquity of cooperation as a force of survival. It was there in the ancient bacteria that joined in permanent symbiosis to create the complex membrane-bound eukaryotic cell of which all plants and animals are made; in flocking birds; in schooling fishes; in Larry Bird's Celtics; in the single fertilized egg as it multiplies, divides, and differentiates, organizing over the course of nine months into the amazing structure of the human body; in the temporary and fragile construction that is family.

Life mutated for the same reason that Hopis deliberately mar their art. From flaw comes the divine spark
that escapes extinction. But for individuals and species,
death was certain. Embedded in the rocks of the canyon
walls were fossil remains of multi-celled sea creatures—
trilobites, corals, and worms. The acrid stench of oil seeping from the rocks spoke of the once lush swamps through
which Tyrannosaurs roamed. The petroglyphs told of the
Anasazi people, long vanished. Jane was gone too.

A week before she died, I had gone to the grocery
store with Dad, buying food that she loved. Jane ate one
small piece of bittersweet chocolate but, with a tube in
her nose and a canister of oxygen, didn't have much appetite. She walked the hospital's hallway, pausing every
few steps to regain her strength, speaking to every nurse,
patient, doctor, and visitor, as if it would be morally wrong
to leave the planet without extending her love to everyone on it. But after ten minutes, she was exhausted and
returned to bed.

"This is my daughter," she introduced me to the
doctor who examined the tea-colored fluid that drained
from her lungs. As he diplomatically explained that the
machine was filling up faster than he wished, Jane faded
from big and little futures—Charlie and Trish's wedding,
Jeremy riding without training wheels, Nathaniel speaking clearly. Jane showed no fear for the journey that she
faced alone. Although she was an estate lawyer whose
job was to help the living prepare for this inescapable
moment, I never suspected that she would be so artful in
managing her own.

When he left, I said, "That's the first time you've
called me your daughter."

"I never wanted to take you away from your
mother," Jane's voice labored.

"You didn't." Tears welled in my eyes, as I fumbled
to reassure her that no one, nothing, not even a linear

accelerator could break the crazy bonds between mother and child. I was lucky enough to have two. Jane met my gaze with a steady absolving one of her own.

I looked up at the blood-red cliffs of the canyon. Filled with a sense of belonging to the same bewildering, sense-defying forces of nature that shaped the river, gulches, and mesa, I had a sudden urge to snap the leash of gravity, to float like the drink cans inside the mesh bag attached to the raft. Ted threw me a rope and I jumped into the cool, abrasive murk.

"Row, row, row your boat," Ted sang.

Nathaniel startled from his sleep as Mom sang off-pitch and Jeremy chimed in with rambunctious energy.

Everyday I make my Lunch.
I get so hungry that I
eat two sandwiches.
Some times I eat three.

# Chapter Thirteen

∽

# Afterword

1999

*T*wice, shortly after death, Jane visited my dreams, suffused with joy and reassurance that she was fine, forbidding me to worry. Aunt EJ completed Jane's unfinished square. The quilt now hangs in our hallway, a memorial to that time in our lives.

Ganny died at the age of ninety-seven. Just before Christmas, she entered the hospital and a week later, surrounded by family, ready to go, her heart stopped.

Jane and Ganny's immortality grew out of the little bits of difference that they made during their lives. But after death, their spirits came back frequently. Jane returned whenever I wore her clothes, particularly the Christmas sweater whose shape shifted to accommodate my broad shoulders. Ganny never appeared in my dreams, perhaps because she lurked everywhere else: in my mother's and aunts' hand-writing, in furniture and rugs that I inherited, and especially in our new house.

We moved to a town not far from Cambridge and bought a house remarkably like my grandmother's—set in a hillside with open California grace. In fact, when my brothers teased at times that I had become my grandmother, I did not argue. My fate was to pick up where she left off.

Charlie bought our Cambridge house but decided our new one was a perfect place for his wedding. Nathaniel got momentarily confused on the day that Charlie married Trish. "Who did you think he was going to marry?" I asked. Nathaniel answered: "Us!"

It made sense. I had wanted to marry Charlie when I was child. Stranger equated danger then.

Dad married again and when I wore Jane's high heels to the wedding, I sensed that she approved not only my outfit but the match. Sarah was a friend of hers; quite literally the woman next door.

My stepfather continued to collect gold balls from tennis tournaments until he finally had to give up the game at the age of ninety-seven, a loss made more painful by the fact that few people showed much sympathy. Harvard Medical School gerontologists studied Ferd, hoping to uncover the secrets of longevity. If the very young and the very old qualify as miracles, then, I wondered, what happens to us during those years in-between?

From Mom, I learned the simple lesson that 90 percent of success in life is a matter of showing up with the right attitude; wearing the right clothes often takes care of the rest. She claimed the grand in grandmother with flair but no longer rushed to eradicate the pain that she saw in her children's lives. She blamed Nathaniel for the fact that her once salt-and-pepper hair had turned completely gray. But she also credited him for ending her fear of flying. He worked in the same counterintuitive way that amphetamines affect hyperactive children.

Nancy Burson had a show in New York City when Nathaniel was one and a half years old. It included not only her photographs but an anomaly machine where you could change your own face. Nancy invited her subjects—including our family—to a celebration party at the opening. Nearly everyone at the gallery had some sort of facial difference and the simple fact of being the majority erased the boundaries between normal and abnormal even more powerfully than Nancy's photos. The weirdest looking person at the opening was a visitor who wore a fashionable outfit. Her skin was lacquered with makeup, every hair anchored in place, all bones in the usual layout. As she viewed Nancy's photographs and tried the anomaly machine, her face twisted into an expression so tainted, lifeless, and full of disease that I was repulsed. The true magic was in the anomaly machine—children with a craniofacial condition glimpsed themselves momentarily without one, while parents without a condition saw themselves with their child's syndrome.

Not long after Nancy's show, I showed her photographs to a class of first-year medical students. They were in a joint degree program, M.D.-Ph.D., which meant that they would do basic research in addition to clinical practice. The teacher introduced the subject of craniofacial deformities by holding up a plastic skull, identifying the six sutures, locating the mid-face and supra-orbital rims, and explaining retrusion, fusion, and lack of bone development. Then he flashed the awful medical mug shots.

I looked around the room, wanting to shout: these medical photos have one purpose—to heighten and intensify difference for a diagnosis. Never confuse the stark facts of science with the people you treat. And if you ever dare think of anyone with these conditions as abnormal then just remember that by virtue of the test scores required by Harvard Medical School, so are you.

Seeing one student with pink punk hair, I calmed down. The rarity of Apert, Crouzon, Treacher-Collins, Boston-type craniosynostosis practically guaranteed that the syndromes would be names to memorize for an exam. How many people with craniofacial conditions would these young doctors-to-be actually meet? For ultimately, this is how social change occurs—by the intersections of lives, in the workplace, school, and home.

Instead, I talked about the people at Nancy's gallery opening who had changed my life: the identical twins from Florida both born with Apert syndrome and how they were loved by their hip teenage brothers; a charismatic kid named Andrew whose amniotic band syndrome had given him a face that Picasso might have painted; a father and daughter both born with Crouzon syndrome who exuded a comfort and acceptance that became my dream.

∾

It did get harder, not easier, to bring Nathaniel back to Children's. Throwing wish pennies in the fountain, riding the glass elevator, visiting the garden, the ICU, and Eight West, learning that Adam had died, Ming had returned to Taiwan with her internal organs back in place, and Willie had moved away evoked memories that carried a raw mixture of love and hate. But Nathaniel returned regularly for small operations (anything less than a craniectomy) and had check-ups with a roster of specialists that expanded as the years passed: an audiologist, cardiologist, dentist, geneticist, ophthalmologist, orthopedist, orthodontist, otolaryngologist, developmental pediatrician, psychologist, craniofacial surgeon, neurosurgeon, hand surgeon, oral surgeon, and anesthesiologist. Some visits took place every three months. Some only in the operating room. The hand surgeon did one exam on the ferryboat to Long Island. (We both happened to be going to visit relatives.) But most of the team greeted Nathaniel at the once a year reunion with Dr. Mulliken presiding over the give-and-take.

Nathaniel would need more craniofacial surgery eventually, but as long as Dr. Mulliken was content to wait, so were we.

"We used to do the mid-face at four," he explained. "Now the studies suggest that early surgery may actually stop the bones from growing. If the mid-face is done early, it certainly has to be redone. So the later, the better. Ten or twelve years old. Wait and see."

"Will you be around?" I asked with hope. Dr. Mulliken was in his late fifties, still boundlessly energetic.

"I'm still figuring out ways to do this better," he laughed. "Tessier's still in the OR."

"Not actually doing the surgery?" I gasped. How steady is anyone's hand at seventy?

"No, just calling the shots," he replied.

"We hope you're here," Ted said.

"They can't get rid of me that easily," Dr. Mulliken said, thinking no doubt of growing deficits at teaching hospitals, like Children's.

The holes in Nathaniel's skull stayed open. We watched them closely, calling before going to Costa Rica one year to ask what if an encephalitis-carrying mosquito bit Nathaniel on the top of his head where the bone was missing. After calculating the length of the mosquito's proboscis and the thickness of the epidermis and dura, the specialists had concluded that he would be safe.

Shortly after Nathaniel's surgeries stopped, Ted's resumed. He had an operation for a hernia, and then several procedures on his knee. After the humane, family-centered experience at Children's, I found adult hospitals to be needlessly cruel. Why couldn't I accompany

Ted into the operating room and hold his hand in recovery? Adults require support as much as kids.

Between his operations, Ted found time and energy to take new risks, which included launching a hedge fund that nobody outside or inside the investment business quite understood. I took my name off law school waiting lists, saying farewell to the mediator I had hoped to be and took care of the children, ran the household, and wrote. Our family joined a Quaker Meeting.

When Magic Johnson got AIDs, Larry Bird retired, and Reggie Lewis died suddenly, basketball lost its magic. Music took its place. I fell in love with opera. The histrionic bellowing and grand sweep of emotion made sense. So did Ernest Shackleton's understanding that music was essential to survival. As his team of polar explorers drifted helplessly across ice floes, he ordered his men to strip themselves of all unnecessary belongings, but made one exception for a twelve-pound zither banjo.

Ted wanted us to make our own music. After buying a used clarinet and banged-up tenor saxophone, we hired a musician from Estonia who knew American musical culture better than a native. In the evenings, honks, brays, and toots permeated the house. Ted played sax and counted the beat while I played clarinet and arrived at rhythm intuitively. He got frustrated, I got impatient, but we persisted, muddling and united by the desire to make something beautiful together. Because of the obstacles that Nathaniel faced, nothing—not even music—was impossible; the only crime was not to try.

But some things are impossible, even with trying. We hoped to have a third child. After many miscarriages—the hardest being Gabriel at twenty weeks—the sorrow accumulated until my soul fled this world in a way that it never had with Nathaniel. The losses changed Ted, who grew calmer, husbanding his resources to do more with less.

When it became clear that our family was complete, an ordinary life looked ambitious enough and we tried to fill it with small gestures of kindness, savoring the unspectacular responsibilities of helping children grow. Jeremy metamorphosed into an affectionate big brother who channeled his aggressive energy into soccer, tennis, hockey, and other sports, playing with a sense of fairness that one teacher likened to a highly developed system of justice. He understood how bodies worked better than many adults. The fact that they came in all shapes, sizes, and colors was obvious, though he disliked too much attention to his own and was easily hurt by the mere thought that someone might be laughing at him. Still, Jeremy was shocked by sights that he didn't usually see, "Look! Mom!" Jeremy shrieked one day in first grade. "A woman policeman!"

The kids in Jeremy's first grade class seized on slim differences to create a social hierarchy, but it was nothing compared to what happened in middle school. By fifth grade, Jeremy was embarrassed by wearing the wrong clothes. In seventh grade, he became preoccupied with his changing face and body but was proud and protective of Nathaniel, promising to beat up anyone who gave his little brother a hard time about the way he looked. When assigned to write a time-line of positive and negative events in his life, Jeremy mentioned Nathaniel only once—his birth being a high point.

Nathaniel absorbed a charismatic joie de vivre that he exuded. But I believe that his personality had been written in the stars. On his second birthday, he went to Cambridge Montessori Nursery school and moved into the biting phase. We all became proficient in baby-signs and then stopped because Nathaniel's articulation improved. The kids understood him and we did too, most of the time. When Ted didn't, he apologized to Nathaniel and said that his ears did not work very well.

By his third birthday, Nathaniel went to parties, had buddies, struggled to be first in line, brought books for sharing, practiced letters, sang songs, and dreamed of being a backhoe driver when he grew up. It was a measure of time's passage when his teacher greeted our worries with a friendly aren't-you-a-little-crazy head-shake.

"What's amazing is that Nathaniel doesn't even know that he is handicapped!" one step-relative observed during his nursery school years. Her appalled tone obscured the truth that Nathaniel was, thankfully, ignorant of *his* place in *her* social order but, more importantly, unaware that his bodily differences mattered significantly.

It was at the age of three that Nathaniel expressed his first awareness that his body differed from ours. During Richard Nixon's funeral on TV, Ted and I clenched our fists in a power salute. "My hand can't do that," Nathaniel said quietly. "No, it can't," I said pushing back my own sadness. "But your hand can do this. Let's do it your way." We raised our hands in the air, fingers open.

When Nathaniel was four and Jeremy was seven, the handicapped question came up. Was Nathaniel? Jeremy asked. He coveted the ubiquitous parking places, conveniently located and often empty. No, we answered, those were for people who had difficulty walking. Like Aunt EJ? Jeremy asked. Yes, now that she was older. But was Nathaniel handicapped? Jeremy pressed. Not in our eyes, but Jeremy might hear other people use that word one day.

The irony was that while shunning the label for Nathaniel, I liberally applied it to others. From the moment of birth, perfection was an illusion and for most people, a burden to overcome. All of us had profound disabilities, serious limitations, some more visible than others. In that sense, Nathaniel was one of the lucky ones.

We continued to get freebies, random kindnesses, stories from strangers, questions about what happened and will he be all right, friendly stares and rude gawks, all variations on themes familiar to anyone with a visible difference. One day, on vacation, when Nathaniel was a preschooler, we even discovered a hand-written note under the windshield wiper of the car. "Hi there!! I saw you folks a moment ago on the path returning from my morning hike. I noticed that one of the children unfortunately suffered from certain complications in life. I had just spent a very relaxing and peaceful time alone in the woods and I have to tell you what a beautiful feeling it was to see all of you together, as what I took to be a family. I was very touched by the sense of caring I felt as we passed by. At first, I felt sadness for the younger child that he could not be as healthy as most children but then I felt a happiness about the love and caring given to a child who needs it. Children really are a blessing, aren't they?"

The unexpected kindness of strangers made it possible to perform the trick required in a prejudiced culture—and that was to not become prejudiced oneself. To the extent possible, we did not want Nathaniel to internalize the 'otherness' imposed on him but to grow up healthy, happy, and deep down, not particularly interested in the opinions of others, except to persuade them to his point of view. So we read books on how to inoculate a child against prejudice, encouraged Nathaniel's friendship with Torrey, and every summer hosted a party for families affected by facial difference in the Boston area.

By and large, school was a safe zone. The birthday party invitations—those talismans of social desirability—came. Nathaniel was comfortable with people and made friends easily. In unsafe zones where people did not know Nathaniel, nothing usually happened. But every now and then, at a museum, playground, or party, an adult would shy away or a kid would wrinkle her nose and point. We tried to educate before exploding and reading anyone the riot act. He was born with his face just the way you were born with yours. His face was not weird. His hands were not bad. Merely different.

It's hard to say exactly when the syndrome ceased to be the center of our lives or Nathaniel's, but the transition was complete by the time he started kindergarten. In fact, a name-change marked the shift. "I want to be called Nate," Nathaniel said. As Nate's abilities eclipsed his difficulties, our worries normalized. Although he had dyslexia and other learning differences, Nate took to school like a bird to the breeze, working with cheerful perseverance. He was compassionate, eager to help those in need, whether it was his Hungarian classmate, hospitalized Daddy, or new baby cousin, Charlie and Trish's daughter. He played soccer, hockey, and baseball, practiced tae kwon do and rode horseback, ignoring what his hands could not do and in that process, discovering what they could.

While ignoring Nate's differences was essential, completely denying them was not. Nate needed to know right from the start that many paradoxical threads make up our identities; no easy task when children tend to seek simple explanations. As Dale Berra once said when asked if he took after his famous father, Yogi: "Nope, all our similarities are different."

Nate was in third grade when he asked in the car one day, "Why did my fingers grow together when I was inside you? Why didn't Jeremy's fingers?"

"You've heard of DNA?" I asked. He nodded and I continued my talk on genetics. "It's like a book of instructions on how to make a human body. In your instructions, there was a tiny spelling mistake. Like spelling REN instead of RUN. That teeny, tiny little mistake gave you the syndrome. You know how easy it is to make a spelling mistake? Everyone has one. Daddy and I do. Jeremy does. You just can't see ours."

We taught him about bones and how they grow. I talked to his classmates, bringing the plaster model of Nathaniel's original hand, a copy of Nancy's book, *Faces,* and a photo album of others with the syndrome. At the beginning of each school year, we sent a letter home.

In third grade, Nate wrote his own: "I don't really like to talk about Apert syndrome because it's not a big deal. If you have questions you can ask me once a week but not twice a week. It's more fun to talk about something else like what to play on the playground or what we do for homework. Apert syndrome is not the most important part of me. I know a lot of other people who have it. It's okay to stare for a short time in a friendly way. Sometimes kids have a hard time understanding me when I speak. Just ask me again and I'll say it slowly. Once I got teased at the playground when my brother was playing soccer. A boy called my head stupid. Kids should not say mean things about each other's bodies. I like to climb trees and eat popsicles."

Seeing begins with believing in the inextricability of heart and bones.

# More Information about Craniofacial Conditions

❧

Apert syndrome is thought to occur in about 1 out of 65,000 to 1 out of 126,000 births in the U.S., but since there is no official registry, these numbers remain an educated guess. Often I cite the incidence as 1 in 100,000 because it's an easy-to-remember, round number. In 1990, the year of Nathaniel's birth, one might expect that somewhere between 16 and 40 other babies born in the United States had the same condition.

A good source of information and support for anyone affected by Apert syndrome can be found on the Internet at **www.Apert.org**

Although most congenital craniofacial conditions are rare, facial differences are not. In fact, each year about 500,000 people are affected as a result of accidents, burns, disease, and congenital conditions such as cleft lip and palate. **About Face** (1-800-665-FACE) is a non-profit organization that provides information, emotional support, and educational programs for and on behalf of individuals with craniofacial anomalies and other disfiguring facial conditions. The founder's advice: "When you stare, stare with a smile."

As for special needs and handicapping conditions . . . check out the NBA.

# Recent Research
# on Apert Syndrome

In 1906, French pediatrician Eugene Apert published a paper in which he described the rare bony malformation that now bears his name. Little was known in Apert's day about what caused this condition and how it might be passed on. He certainly noticed its spontaneous and sporadic occurrence and he may have observed that adults with the syndrome sometimes had children likewise affected. But the tools available to him sharply limited further understanding.

Nearly 100 years later, the story of Apert syndrome is unfolding, aided by advances in biotechnology. In 1995, Dr. Andrew Wilkie and his research team in Cambridge, England, announced that they had discovered the gene for Apert syndrome. Scientists currently believe that there are approximately 100,000 genes in every cell in the human body. Although the Human Genome Project is in the process of mapping these genes, locating one gene that causes a specific condition is still difficult, akin to stumbling across a grain of rice in the Astrodome.

Now we know that Apert syndrome is caused by a gene mutation that results in an altered cellular receptor protein. The receptor is known as Fibroblast Growth Factor Receptor 2 (FGFR2). It spans the cell's membrane, but the receptor is located on the outside of many cells, including bone cells. Its job is to mediate the response of cells to FGF, one of many external signals that control cell growth and differentiation. A single amino acid mistake—a substitution of one amino acid for another—in this receptor protein results in the bony malformations of craniosynostosis and syndactyly that characterize Apert syndrome. The intriguing question is how?

The details about Apert syndrome will be filled in with time because many other skeletal disorders, including the more commonly occurring conditions of dwarfism, are caused by slightly different mutations in the same family of receptors. Because Apert syndrome is a unique phenotype associated with what many researchers call "an exquisitely specific" mutation—a rare thing itself in the field of genetics—it offers an unusual window into the fascinating and complex process of how the human body is assembled. The Fibroblast Growth Factors and their receptors are also an important family of intercellular signaling molecules, involved not only in embryological development but also in wound healing and tumor growth.

## Intercellular Signaling: Fibroblast Growth Factors and Their Receptors

The last decade has witnessed an explosion of research on Fibroblast Growth Factors and their receptors. The field, which attracts cancer researchers as well as those interested in the riddles of development, has been characterized by a rapid rate of discovery, unexpected findings, and some degree of confusion. The Fibroblast Growth Factors (FGFs) and their receptors (FGFRs) are a family of important intercellular signaling molecules. They play a critical role in development, beginning at the earliest stages of vertebrate embryogenesis. They initiate the whole program of limb development and are responsible for inducing/regulating the development of most organs in the vertebrate body. After development, they are involved in cell growth and cell differentiation, and, depending on the target cell, wound healing and tumor growth.

## Apert Syndrome Mutation

The mutation that causes Apert syndrome occurs in the portion of FGFR2 that binds with the growth factor. The receptor mutation primarily affects the development of the craniofacial and skeletal systems in utero but also throughout the bone-growing years of childhood. The mutation is not deleterious enough to be lethal to the embryo. While the specific molecular mechanisms are not known at this time, the end-result is that the receptor is activated in the presence of smaller amounts of growth factor than normal.

There are 23 pairs of chromosomes in the nucleus of most cells in the human body. The gene that codes for FGFR2 is located on chromosome 10. Genes are composed of DNA, which in turn is composed of the four nucleotide bases—adenine, thymine, guanine, and cytosine. The sequence of these bases determines the structure of proteins such as the receptor involved in Apert syndrome: FGFR2.

The Apert syndrome mutation is caused by a transversion in the DNA, or what can be seen as a simple spelling mistake. In a specific location on chromosome 10, where a cytosine should be, guanine is present instead. This mistake in turn affects the sequence of amino acids in the receptor protein.

The receptor protein is composed of a long strand of hundreds of amino acids. The Apert mutation occurs at one of two places in that strand. The more common of the two, which occurs 70 percent of the time, is found at amino acid #252, where a tryptophan is substituted for a serine. The other mutation occurs at amino acid #253, where arginine is substituted for proline.

These mutations typically arise spontaneously and in the case of new mutations, they arise in the sperm. For the individual affected by Apert syndrome, however, the mutation is autosomal dominant, which means that he or she has a 50/50 chance of passing the syndrome to offspring.

## Craniosynostosis

What has been clearly shown is the way that this mutation leads to craniosynostosis, or premature fusion of sutures in the skull. Consider normal cranial suture development. The cranium is composed of several bony plates that meet and grow together at junctions called sutures. The major sutures are coronal, sagittal, lambdoid, and metopic. The suture is composed of two plates of bone separated by a space filled with immature, rapidly dividing osteogenic stem cells. These "preosteoblasts" differentiate into osteoblasts, or bone-forming cells. The osteoblasts synthesize and secrete the material that eventually mineralizes into bone.

In normal development, the sutures do not fuse until a child is about a year old. This allows the bony plates to move as the baby's head passes through the birth canal and also gives the rapidly growing brain a way to expand in the first year of life. In craniosynostosis, one, two, or three of the major sutures of the skull fuse prematurely in utero. A group of researchers in Paris led by Dr. Lomri demonstrated in 1998 that the Apert mutation causes premature bone cell differentiation in the skull.

The bone cells grew normally but the rate at which preosteoblastic cells matured into osteoblasts was elevated in those with Apert syndrome. The mutation induced cells to become bone-forming cells too early and this led to premature fusion of the cranial sutures.

## Hands and Feet

In Apert syndrome, the hands and feet can be mildly to severely affected. Typically, the webbing (syndactyly) is symmetrical and fingers are foreshortened due to missing bones (carpals) in the fingers. In mild cases, the bones and soft tissues of the second, third, and fourth fingers are fused—while thumb and pinky are separate. In severe cases, the hand resembles a rosebud, with fingers all pulled together. The feet follow the mildness or severity of the hands. Many people have noticed, anecdotally, that those with more severely affected hands and feet often have more mildly affected midfaces. And vice versa—those with more severely affected midfaces have mildly affected hands and feet.

Two groups of researchers tested the hypothesis that each hand shape (phenotype) might be related to a single gene but got conflicting results. The question endures: why should two mutations, located in adjacent amino acids, each produce a distinct phenotype? This question will be explored further, since FGFR2 receptor is clearly involved in both digital and craniofacial development in utero.

Apert syndrome is one of many skeletal disorders, including dwarfism, that involve mutations in the FGFR family. Most of these FGFR mutations are missense—that is, resulting in a single amino acid substitution. They all appear to work by the same activation of intercellular signals. The similarities between the mutations and the disorders suggest that the four FGFRs have overlapping functions related to the control of bone growth. Achondroplasia, the most common form of dwarfism, results from a mutation in FGFR3 which leads to the premature restraint of chondrocyte proliferation in the bones.

## Future Research

Within the near future, researchers expect to create a mouse that has the Apert syndrome mutation in order to answer some of these key questions. The answers will help not only those affected but all those interested in better understanding how the human body forms and maintains itself. For affected individuals, one outcome of this research is that it is now possible to test for Apert syndrome in utero, which offers a choice to individuals who wish to have children.

## Literature Cited

Apert, E. De l'acrocephalosyndactylie. **Bull. Mem. Soc. Med. Hop. Paris** 23: 1310-1330, 1906.

Basilico, C. and Moscatelli, D. The FGF family of growth factors and oncogenes. **Advances in Cancer Research** 52: 115-165, 1992.

Burke, D., Wilkes, D., Blundell, T., and Malcolm, S. Fibroblast growth factor receptors: lessons from the genes. **Trends in Biochemical Sciences** 23: 59-62, 1998.

Lomri, A., Lemonnier, J., Hott, M., De Parseval, N., Lajeunie, E., Munnick, A., Renier, D., and Marie, P. Increased calvaria cell differentiation and bone matrix formation induced by fibroblast growth factor receptor 2 mutations in Apert syndrome. **The Journal of Clinical Investigation** 101 (6): 1310-1317, 1998.

Martin, G. The role of FGFs in the early development of the vertebrate limbs. **Genes and Development** 12: 1571-1586. 1998.

Mason, I. The ins and outs of fibroblast growth factors. **Cell** 78: 547-552, 1994.

Moloney, D., Slaney, S., Oldridge, M., Wall, S., Sahlin, P., Stenman, G., and Wilkie, A. Exclusive paternal origin of new mutations in Apert syndrome. **Nature Genetics** 13: 48-53, 1996.

Park, W-J., Theda, C., Maestri, N., Meyers, G., Fryburg, J., Dufresne, C., Cohen, M., and Jabs, E. Analysis of phenotypic features and FGFR2 mutations in Apert syndrome. **American Journal of Human Genetics** 57: 321-328, 1995.

Slaney, S., Oldridge, M., Hurst, J., Moriss-Kay, G., Hall, C., Poole, M., and Wilkie, A. Differential effects of FGFR2 mutations on syndactyly and cleft palate in Apert syndrome. **American Journal of Human Genetics** 58: 923-932, 1996.

Webster, M. and Donoghue, D. FGFR activation in skeletal disorders: too much of a good thing. **Trends in Genetics** 13 (5): 178-182, 1997.

Wilkie, A. Craniosynostosis: genes and mechanisms. **Human Molecular Genetics** 6 (10): 1647-1656, 1997.

Wilkie, A., Slaney, S., Oldridge, M., Poole, M., Ashworth, G., Hockley, A., Hayward, R., David, D., Pulleyn, L., Rutland, P., Malcolm, S., Winter, R., and Reardon, W. Apert syndrome results from localized mutations of FGFR2 and is allelic with Crouzon syndrome. **Nature Genetics** 9: 165-177, 1995.